Ten Service Plans
for
Contemporary
Worship

Ron Rienstra

FAITH
ALIVE®
Christian Resources

CRC Publications
Grand Rapids, Michigan

Calvin Institute of Christian Worship
Grand Rapids, Michigan

Unless otherwise indicated, Scripture quotations in this publication are from the Holy Bible, New Revised Standard Version, © 1989, Division of Christian Education of the National Council of Churches of Christ in the United States of America. Used by permission of Zondervan Publishing House.

Ten Service Plans for Contemporary Worship is copublished by Faith Alive Christian Resources, a ministry of CRC Publications (orders@faithaliveresources.org; www.FaithAliveResources.org), and the Calvin Institute of Christian Worship, 3201 Burton SE, Grand Rapids, MI 49546 (worship@calvin.edu; www.calvin.edu/worship).

We welcome your comments. Call us at 1-800-333-8300 or e-mail us at editors@faithaliveresources.org.

Library of Congress Cataloging-in-Publication Data
Rienstra, Ron, 1965-
   Ten service plans for contemporary worship / Ron Rienstra.
     p. cm.
   ISBN 1-56212-868-X
   1. Worship programs. I. Title.
BV198.R56 20002
264—dc21

2002015722

10 9 8 7 6 5 4 3 2

Contents

Introduction

Some terms become hopelessly confusing as soon as they gain wide use. *Contemporary worship* is one of them. For most folks, the term has become shorthand for worship that is informed and shaped by contemporary cultural sensibilities, primarily musical. Other such sensibilities include the predominance of expressive praise; a few singers rather than a choir; a presentational leadership style; a desire for Spirit-led spontaneity; an evangelistic motivation; and an emphasis on the visual rather than the verbal, on intuition and feeling rather than words and linear thought. But in its strictest sense, contemporary worship means worship—in whatever style—that is offered *now* as opposed to way back when. So to call the service plans in this book contemporary is somewhat misleading. Yes, they presume amplified instruments and familiarity with music composed in the past generation or so. But they are historical and somewhat *un*contemporary in the sense that they are based on worship services offered to God at least two years ago at the LOFT, the student-led Sunday evening service at Calvin College.

Some of what we do at Calvin College—and some of what is presented here—is indeed up-to-the-minute. On the other hand, students, like anyone else, need stability and connection. And as our Orthodox brothers and sisters teach us, the worship of the church does not, in the end, belong to us. It began long before us and will continue after we are gone. Good contemporary worship, it seems to me, follows the wisdom of ancient patterns, yet gives these patterns a fresh voice. It adapts older material, gratefully accepting and gently transforming tradition. And it welcomes new material from a variety of sources, placing things fittingly into the basic flow of worship. In the services presented here, that "flow" is largely determined by music. We move through the liturgy's contours by singing one song after another. Then we give shape and direction to our singing with transitions, spoken prayers, readings from Scripture, and so on.

HOW TO USE THIS COLLECTION

The services in this book are presented in the form of structured notes (see below). Each service has a particular theme and a specific Bible text at its heart, and each generally follows a classic threefold pattern for worship: Gathering as God's People, Hearing the Word, and Responding to the Word. That basic structure is further broken down into worship activities—usually labeled with "tion" words: *celebration, lamentation, dedication,* and so on. This reminds us that worship isn't just twenty minutes before the "talk"; it isn't a magical, metaphorical, musical journey into God's lap. Rather it is an active, dramatic exercise, a dynamic dialogue between God and God's people. On those occasions when we make use of a different pattern, the form still centers on the proclamation of the Word. Within these supportive structures, we strive to plan and enact services that exhibit qualities I have come to believe are essential to good worship (see p. 9).

Liturgical Notes
These indicate supplemental Scripture passages, prayers, and notes on spoken transitions. Sometimes a word-for-word transition or prayer is suggested; in other cases, I only shoot arrows in a direction I hope is helpful, and leave individual worship leaders to chase them down.

While you're chasing, remember three things:

(1) Good transitions use words that point backward to what's just happened (key words from the Scripture just read) and forward to what's about to happen (lyrics from the next song).

(2) Good transitions avoid inserting the self (as in "I'd like you to stand up to sing . . ." or "Lord, I want to pray for . . .").

(3) The best transitions always *invite* or encourage (rather than instruct) the congregation to enter into the next act of worship—confession, adoration, dedication, and so on.

Finally, because each service is centered in the proclaimed Word, sermon notes are included where at all possible.

Musical Notes

These offer practical suggestions for arranging songs and making transitions between songs so the service flows. They are by no means the last and best word on how to do a particular song. They are merely one way to perform a song in order to support its purpose in a particular liturgical context.

These notes presume a basic "band": singer(s), a keyboard, a bit of hand percussion, and at least one guitar (in tune, please). At the college we are blessed with an embarrassment of gifted musicians, so our band is rather large: a piano and an electronic keyboard, three guitars (acoustic, electric, and bass), a drum kit (sometimes called a trap set), some hand percussion, a small singing ensemble (two to six people), and perhaps a solo instrument or two (saxophone, flute, violin). Even so, these notes should be helpful whether your worship leadership team has three or thirty-three members.

Read these service notes with a guitar or piano nearby. Play and speak through the transitions, noting what is going on inside you intellectually, emotionally, and spiritually. Feel free to jot comments and suggestions for yourself on the pages.

Finally . . .

An important point: despite the use of the imperative mood (for stylistic reasons), these service plans are not prescriptive. They are merely a jumping-off point for your own reflection and Spirit-led creative preparation. Don't follow every suggestion in detail. Preachers will hear something different in a given text that is God's Word for their time and place. Musicians and liturgists too should amend and adjust for their particular congregation. Add a litany, replace one song with one your congregation knows better, and so on. Do so with sensitivity and attention most of all to the *purpose* of a given liturgical element.

Finally, I would like to acknowledge the contributions of my predecessors at the LOFT—Gregg DeMey and Gregory Kett—and my assistants these past years: Peter Armstrong, Nathan Cole, Molly Delcamp, Jillayne Kelder, and especially Aaron Genzink. Besides these, there are too many other students to name who helped to plan and lead these services. Their creativity and commitment has made LOFT a marvelous learning experience—for them and for me—and a blessing for the entire college community. And, we hope, to God.

Good Contemporary Worship Is . . .

- **Covenantal.** Services are a *conversation* between God and God's people in which we renew the covenant of grace.
- **Participative.** Worship leaders are not performers but *enablers* encouraging the full, conscious, active participation of the congregation (not "audience").
- **Holistic.** We bring all of ourselves to worship: old and young, body and soul, brain and heart, doubt and belief, lament and joy.
- **Expansive.** We make creative use of words, music—and more!—from many times, places, peoples, and cultures to enlarge our vision of God's kingdom and situate ourselves properly within it.
- **Reverent.** Even when playful, our worship acknowledges that we deal with a mysterious God when we gather together.
- **Spirit-directed.** We are led by the Holy Spirit in form and in freedom, both in prayer-filled planning and in the surprising moments of worship.
- **Expectant.** The Spirit blows where it will, so we worship with our sails raised, expecting great things of God and enjoying, rather than engineering, a contagious spiritual energy.

Music Sources

One of the fundamental principles that sustains our worship at the LOFT is that a balanced musical diet is crucial for spiritual health. Finding the resources for such balance doesn't require an entire shelf of hymnals and songbooks. A few select purchases, within the reach of even the most modest church budget, is all it takes. The songs chosen in this collection have been edited so that the vast majority of songs come from three primary sources:

- *Psalter Hymnal.* © 1987 CRC Publications, 2850 Kalamazoo SE, Grand Rapids, MI 49560.
- *Sing! A New Creation* Leader's edition. © 2002, jointly published by Faith Alive Christian Resources, a ministry of CRC Publications; the Calvin Institute of Christian Worship; and the Reformed Church in America.
- Praise & Worship trilogy (which all come in a handful of editions, including the Piano/Guitar/Vocal edition [the one I use], the Worship Planner edition, the Keyboard Edition, the Instrumental edition, and more):

  Songs for Praise & Worship. © 1992 Word Music
  More Songs for Praise & Worship. © 2000 Word Music
  More Songs for Praise & Worship 2. © 2002 Word Music

In addition to these, the following are the other musical resources referenced in this volume.

- *City on a Hill, Songs of Worship and Praise.* © 2000 MM Brentwood-Benson Music Publishing, Inc., 741 Cool Springs Blvd., Franklin, TN 37067.
- *Gather Comprehensive* Accompaniment edition. © 1994, GIA Publications, 7404 South Mason Ave., Chicago, IL 60638.
- *Hillsong Music Collection* Vol. 2. © 1999. Website: www.hillsong.com. Orders: sales@hillsong.com.
- *Libro de Liturgia y Cántico.* © 1998, Augsburg Fortress. The Spanish-language hymnal of the Evangelical Lutheran Church in America.

- *Maranatha! Music Praise Chorus Book* Third edition. © 1993 Maranatha! Music. Word/Maranatha, 3319 West End Ave., Nashville, TN 37203.
- *Maranatha! Music Praise Chorus Book* Fourth edition. © 1997 Maranatha! Music. A Division of the Corinthian Group.
- *Mil Voces para celebrar.* © 1996 Abingdon Press. Spanish-language hymnal of the United Methodist Church.
- *Shout to the Lord! Kids 2.* Integrity Music. Website: www.integritymusic.com. Orders: cservice@integinc.com.
- *Songs.* Young Life, compiled by Yohan Anderson. © 1993 Songs and Creations Inc., P.O. Box 7, San Anselmo, CA 94960. 800-227-2188.
- *Songs for LiFE.* © 1994 CRC Publications, 2850 Kalamazoo Ave. SE, Grand Rapids, MI 49560. 800-333-8300.
- *Songs of the Vineyard* vol. 2, 3, 4. © 1994 Vineyard Music Group. Mercy/Vineyard Publishing. Administered by Music Services, 209 Chappelwood Dr., Franklin, TN 37064. 615-794-9015.
- *This Far by Faith.* © 1999 Augsburg Fortress, P.O. Box 1209, Minneapolis, MN 55440-1209.
- *Trinity Hymnal.* © 1990 Great Commission Publications, Inc. 7401 Old York Rd., Philadelphia, PA 19126.
- *Worship and Praise Songbook.* © 1999 Augsburg Fortress. 800-328-4648.
- *Worship Today: Songs & Hymns for the Whole Church.* © 2001 Spring Harvest. Website: springharvest.org. Orders: orders@worshiptoday.co.uk.

Finally, a few children's songs we have no music to, we simply know them.

- "I've Got the Joy"
- "Jesus Loves the Little Children"
- "Arky/Rise and Shine"

The song "I Cannot Come" is actually "The Wedding Banquet." It can be found in the album *Joy Is Like the Rain,* © 1966, Medical Mission Sisters, 77 Sherman Street, Hartford, CT 06105-2260. mms@hartsem.edu.

Abbreviations

City on a Hill, Songs of Worship and Praise (CH)

Gather Comprehensive (GC)

Hillsong Music Collection (HMC)

Libro de Liturgia y Cántico (LLC)

Maranatha! Music Praise Chorus Book Third edition (MMP3)

Maranatha! Music Praise Chorus Book Fourth edition (MMP4)

Mil Voces para celebrar (MV)

More Songs for Praise & Worship (MSPW)

More Songs for Praise & Worship 2 (MSPW2)

Psalter Hymnal (PsH)

Shout to the Lord! Kids 2 (SLK2)

Sing! A New Creation (SNC)

Songs Young Life (SYL)

Songs for LiFE (SFL)

Songs for Praise & Worship (SPW)

Songs of the Vineyard vol. 2, 3, 4 (SV2, SV3, SV4)

This Far by Faith (TFF)

Worship & Praise Songbook (WPS)

Worship Today: Songs & Hymns for the Whole Church (WT)

Are You Listening?

1 Samuel 3; Psalm 95

In the central Scripture for this service, Samuel is surprised to hear God speaking *directly to him.* From start to finish, through repeated use of Scripture and phrases like "The Word of the Lord," this service explores the conviction that God will speak to us if we are attentive listeners. The opening musical "set" is structured around the first 7 verses of Psalm 95, and is meant to be as seamless as possible. While there is only a little silence before the sermon, afterward there is significant time for listening prayer and for dedicating ourselves to listening more and then to doing whatever God will have whispered to us.

CONGREGATION

Liturgical Notes: The service begins in silence. If there is noisy fellowship at the start of the service, the worship leader can step up to a microphone, Bible in hand, and await everyone's attention. When it has been silent for at least five seconds, the leader says: "Listen to the Word of the Lord!"

[Scripture verses from Psalm 95 can be displayed via overhead or PowerPoint.]

6 O come, let us worship and bow down, let us kneel before the LORD, our Maker! **7** For he is our God, and we are the people of his pasture, and the sheep of his hand.

Musical Notes: When the leader has read the verses, begin an introduction for "Come Let Us Worship and Bow Down" (SPW 246). Key of D. Accompany with a full band at a bright tempo (no slower than 100 bpm). Aim for a tone of confident praise, not pastoral repose or majestic awe. Sing twice through with a slight ritard at the end.

CELEBRATION

Liturgical Notes: When song concludes, the leader again says: "The Word of the Lord," and then reads these verses from Psalm 95:

1 O come, let us sing to the LORD; let us make a joyful noise to the rock of our salvation! **2** Let us come into his presence with thanksgiving; let us make a joyful noise to him with songs of praise!

Musical Notes: While the leader declares the next Word of the Lord from the psalm (above), the band—or as much of it as is able, perhaps only the piano—makes a transition into the key of Em. Ending in D, walk the bass down to C, then play Bsus, then B7, then Em. Try to time the transition so you hit the Em chord exactly as the leader finishes. Add the percussion and guitars immediately to set the tempo for "Cantad al Señor" (SNC 224). Key of Em. Sing with exuberance and passion, in English or Spanish, or both at the same time—a joyful noise is fine with God! Vary the accompaniment from stanza to stanza. For instance, add an instrument on each repetition of the first line to build into "sing to our God." Add a trumpet on stanza 3. On stanza 4 (shout to our God), crescendo to the shout and then let the instruments (except percussion) fade down, only to build again toward the next "shout"—encourage actual shouting. Add lots of percussion—maracas, claves, tambourine and hand drum at least. Play briskly, one beat per measure (dotted quarter at 60 bpm). Sing the first stanza again at the end with a big ritard.

ADORATION

Liturgical Notes: As song concludes, leader says, "The Word of the Lord!" and then reads verses 3-6:

3 The LORD is a great God, and a great King above all gods. *4* In his hand are the depths of the earth; the heights of the mountains are his also. *5* The sea is his, for he made it, and the dry land, which his hands have formed. *6* O come, let us worship and bow down, let us kneel before the LORD, our Maker!

Musical Notes: Underneath the reading (above), make a simple transition from Em to E. Then the guitar can begin playing an intro to the next song, ending on a sustained B chord to cue the congregation's singing of "Lord Most High" (SNC 18). Key of E. Sing antiphonally, men and women, or divide the congregation in half. Try to create the sense of widening circles of praise—from the corners of the sanctuary and the ends of the earth. Conclude with a gentle decrescendo and ritard, moving without pause into 4/4 time and the introduction to "Come, Let us Worship and Bow Down." This time in the key of E. Play the introduction underneath the reading of Scripture.

Liturgical Notes: Leader says, "The Word of the Lord!" and reads verses 6-7:

6 O come, let us worship and bow down, let us kneel before the LORD, our Maker! *7* For he is our God, and we are the people of his pasture, and the sheep of his hand.

O that today you would listen to his voice!

Musical Notes: Sing "Come, Let Us Worship and Bow Down" once through, this time slower, aiming at a sense of God's majesty and presence. Conclude and without pause play introduction for "O Christ, the Lamb of God" (PsH 257). Key of Dm. Play introduction underneath Scripture reading that follows.

CONFESSION

Liturgical Notes: Leader says, "The Word of the Lord!" and reads Isaiah 53:6:

All we like sheep have gone astray; we have all turned to our own way, and the LORD has laid on him the iniquity of us all.

Then leader says something like the following: "We are the sheep of God's pasture. But like real sheep, we wander and get lost; we're stubborn and refuse to do what's best for us. And so God sent to us One who is not only the Good Shepherd, but who became like us: a sheep, a lamb. And we look to that one to save us. Let's pray."

Musical Notes: Congregation sings through the prayer "O Christ, the Lamb of God" once plaintively. To get a sense of our frailty and vulnerability, accompany minimally—a guitar and violin on the first time (when women and children sing), a piano and bassoon or cello on the second (when the men sing), and all on the third time.

REDEMPTION

Musical Notes: The amen at the conclusion of the last song brings the music from the key of Dm to G. Underneath the spoken words (below), the entire band gently plays the introduction to "Alleluia, He Is Coming" (WSV4 10). Key of G. The vocal range for this song may be difficult in this key, we often do it in C.

Liturgical Notes: Leader says, "Listen to the Word of the Lord"; then reads Isaiah 53:5:

But he was wounded for our transgressions, crushed for our iniquities; upon him was the punishment that made us whole, and by his bruises we are healed.

Then leader says something like the following: "We are healed—forgiven. Jesus Christ came to live among us, to suffer with us, to die for us, and to rise again to save us. He's coming again someday, and by the power of the Spirit, he's here *now*, ready to speak to us, to touch us again with love. He is here. Now. Alleluia."

Musical Notes: Sing "Alleluia, He Is Coming" slowly ($\quarternote = 80$), with wonder at Jesus' sacrifice and the mystery of God's presence among us. Support this pace with plenty of rhythmic texture—more on the celebrative stanzas, less on the sorrowing ones. We usually sing five stanzas: (1) saw my Lord a-coming down the road, (2) saw my Lord a-weeping for my sins, (3) saw my Lord a-dying on the cross, (4) heard my Lord a-calling out my name, (5) saw my Lord a-rising from the grave. (Since we're focusing on Christ's presence now, omit the stanza about Christ's coming again in the clouds). Let the intensity ebb and flow freely. After the last stanza, sing the chorus twice, the second time a cappella.

15

The piano (only) comes in again on "he is here" and gently plays introduction to "God Himself Is with Us" (PsH 244). Key of G. Play as starkly as possible on the first stanza to evoke the awe of the temple. An organ accompaniment would not be out of place. Add guitars strumming one chord per measure on the second stanza's "harps." Pull out all the stops on the last stanza.

PREPARATION

Liturgical Notes: When the song concludes, allow for a long moment of silent wonder. Leader offers a prayer like the following: "Mighty God, Great Shepherd, we long to be sheep who recognize your voice and follow where you lead. We long to hear you speak a word to us today. Show yourself; our eyes are open. Speak, Lord, we're listening. Speak, Lord, in the stillness:

"While I wait on thee;
hush my heart to listen
in expectancy.
Speak, O blessed Master
in this quiet hour;
let me see thy face, Lord,
feel thy touch of power."

—1920, May E. Grimes

Musical Notes: After the spoken prayer, an acoustic guitar and a flute play a short introduction for "Open Our Eyes, Lord" (SNC 80). Key of D. Sing through once, prayerfully.

PROCLAMATION

After a few moments of silence, the leader says, "Listen to the Word of the Lord"; then reads 1 Samuel 3:1-10 (or through 4:1).

The sermon follows the contours of the text, asking how we respond to the biblical claim that the Lord, the Maker of heaven and earth, speaks—and speaks to us.

Outline:

1. The Lord speaks—how do you respond to this claim?
2. Is God's Word rare today?
3. Is God calling your name?
   God calls children—those without status or gifts
   God's call is persistent—three times
4. Are you listening?
   It's hard because of the judgment we fear we'll hear.
   It's hard because of the noise in our lives.
   Some practical suggestions for the listening life.
5. Conclusion: Once again, how do you respond to the claim that God is speaking?

After the sermon, the preacher concludes by saying, "Let's pray. Speak, Lord. We're listening." *Long silence follows.* "Amen."

Musical Notes: A solo instrument plays the melody for "Be Still and Know" (SFL 225). Key of C. Play all the way through as introduction. The congregation sings all three stanzas slowly and prayerfully. It's crucial that this song be contemplative and familiar. (Another good option, though less familiar, is "Jesu, tawa pano" (SNC 5). Its theology—"we are here for you" is properly contextualized in this service by prior acknowledgment of God's presence with us.)

INTERCESSION

Liturgical Notes: Minister or other leader offers prayers for the people. An introduction that makes reference to the sung prayer "Be Still and Know" follows: "O Lord, in you we put our trust. When life is good, we trust you; and when life is hard, we try to trust you more. We thank you today for . . .*(prayers of thanksgiving).* And we pray today for *(prayers of intercession)."*

The prayer should be paced slowly to give the congregation a chance to hear what God is speaking to them throughout. Moments of silence would be very appropriate.

Musical Notes: As prayer concludes, band begins introduction to "One Thing I Ask" (WSV2 122). Key of G. Sing this psalmic prayer longingly, lovingly. Change the word *see* to *hear* the second time through the refrain.

DEDICATION

Musical Notes: End the song (above) with an acoustic guitar alternating between a G and a C/G chord, which, at the same tempo, is the introduction for "Here I Am, Lord" (SNC 268). Key of G. Continue this while the leader prays.

Liturgical Notes: The leader prays: "Lord, we desire to see you. So we ask you to open our eyes to your presence in the people around us. Give us hearts and minds and wills that long to serve 'the least of these.' Accept now these gifts, and the lives they represent. Use them to do your work in the world. In Jesus' name, amen."

"Now as we offer our gifts to God, listen for God's voice and join together on the chorus 'Here I am, Lord.'"

Musical Notes: A soloist sings the first stanza, a different soloist the second, and another still the third. The congregation joins together on the chorus. Accompany with an ear toward the humility of Samuel's "Here I am" rather than the majesty of God's "I the Lord of sea and sky."

BENEDICTION

Liturgical Notes: Leader speaks a benediction based on Hebrews 13:20-21: "The Word of the Lord. The God of peace brought our Lord Jesus, the great shepherd of the flock, back again from the dead. May God give you every good gift, that you may do God's will. May our God work within you all that is pleasing in God's sight through Jesus Christ. Glory be to Jesus forever and ever! Amen."

Musical Notes: No concluding song is necessary, but a simple "Amen" song (SNC 286) is a fitting conclusion. Have a leader sing all the way through the short piece once alone. Then lead the congregation into singing as a round in three parts. All conclude on the first two bars repeated until all are singing in unison.

Baptism: Called to Belong to Jesus Christ

Romans 1:1-8

A t LOFT, we don't celebrate the sacrament of baptism. Yet this service and its theme point so clearly in that direction—the direction of God's prevenient grace—that I've amended the service to include a rite of initiation. The song selections do not center in baptismal images (water, purification, and so on), so the service can be used even if you won't be splashing anyone (though you may wish, in such an event, to do something to reaffirm our own baptisms).

The service begins reflectively rather than with boisterous praise. As themes from the sermon are introduced, the praise grows and then flows naturally as we more fully perceive God's goodness. Following the sermon, we offer gifts—and the lives they represent—to Christ, and dedicate ourselves to living joyfully for him. This presents our subjective affirmative response to God's objective yes to us in Jesus Christ and in baptism.

CONGREGATION

Liturgical Notes: God gets the first word in our worship as the leader begins with a greeting from Psalm 121:

1 I lift up my eyes to the hills—from where will my help come?
2 My help comes from the LORD, who made heaven and earth.

Leader continues by saying something like this: "The One who made heaven and earth and called the world into being calls us together to worship. Let's sing to God of our need and his love. Join us."

Musical Notes: Underneath the leader's spoken words (above), a pianist quietly plays gentle arpeggios, alternating between two chords (C and F) in the mood of the first song, but not invoking the melody. The rest of the band is tacit, giving attention to the spoken Word.

As the leader finishes, the piano plays, prayerfully and plaintively, a brief introduction (the first three measures) to "I Lift My Eyes Up" (SNC 208), a partial setting of Psalm 121. Key of C. Bass and drums join (lightly) on first stanza to support the congregation. A solo instrument (violin) doubles the melody. Add a voice in harmony, a third lower, at "My help comes from you." All players join on chorus. Soloists improvise in the rests between sung phrases. End on the dominant chord at the *fine,* then transition into the key of G by playing Am7, D7sus, D7, G.

ADORATION

Liturgical Notes: Leader says something like the following: "We have lifted our eyes, now we lift our hands. This song gives us explicit permission to raise our hands, literally, in a biblically sanctioned act of worship. The middle lines affirm our worship of God alone. The last line presents the theme of this service: 'Unto your name I will bring my sacrifice.'"

Musical Notes: "I Lift My Hands" (WT). Key of G. Move seamlessly from the previous song to this one (no tempo change). Accompany with guitar or piano for the introduction. A solo instrument leads the melody, while another echoes. Sing with earnestness.

Strike two dramatic chords after "measure," then cut out until the downbeat on "heart's desire." Repeat in a similar fashion at "treasure" and "name." Sing twice through, ritard at conclusion.

CONFESSION

Liturgical Notes: Leader prays as follows: "We bring our sacrifice to you today, great God: the gifts of our worship, our lives, our love, our singing, our praying, our playing, our listening, our thinking, our feeling—all these we offer today. For you are great and good and loving. You are holy and righteous and mighty. And because you are, we know that we are sinful. We're lazy, resentful. We resist the lessons you would teach us. We care mostly about ourselves, we don't care that much for others, and we're untrusting of your care for us. We cry out, Lord, for your hand of mercy to heal us. We are bound by sin, and we need your love to free us. You are our strength in weakness. Come rescue us, O Lord."

(The last lines of the prayer anticipate the opening words to the next song, a continuation of the prayer for healing and forgiveness.)

RECONCILIATION

Musical Notes: Sing the first half of "Good to Me" (SNC 71) with a confessional tone. Key of G. The piano only plays a short introduction to maintain continuity with the spoken prayer. Then the musicians may join to thicken the texture and increase intensity. After the repeat, play the musical line "Come rescue me, O Lord" (Em, Bm7, C2) beneath the spoken word of assurance.

Liturgical Notes: Leader speaks with joy this assurance of pardon based on Romans 5: "The proof of God's amazing love for us is this: while we were still sinners, Christ died for us. And if we have died with Christ, we believe that we shall also live with him. So, Paul says, you must also consider yourselves dead to sin and alive to God in Christ Jesus. Jesus, who is our hope, and who promises us that our sins are forgiven!"

Musical Notes: After the declaration of the good news, the second half of the song ("Good to Me") becomes celebrative and jubilant. Give the "for you are good" section a slightly Latin feel with percussion. On the repeating final phrase, the band does not take the repeat, but cycles through "for you are good . . . to me" several times till it ritards into a conclusion.

CELEBRATION

Liturgical Notes: Referring to the last song, the leader says, "God is good!" If the congregation does not respond with an enthusiastic "Amen!" then prompt again. The leader continues with something like the following: "If you all were Baptists, that 'Amen' would be second nature. Whether or not you are all Baptists, most of you are, I suspect, baptized. Despite our many differences, we have a foundational unity in our calling to belong to God in Jesus Christ. That calling is made visible in a sign—the water of baptism."

[Leader may pour water from pitcher into font at this point.]

Leader continues by saying, "In response to God's goodness to us, we sing songs of praise—old, well-loved, rich hymns of praise, and brand-new songs from other lands. Right now we'll sing a new song, and then an old one in new wineskins. God is good! Amen! Alleluia!"

Musical Notes: "Halle, Halle, Halle" (SNC 44). Key of G. An exultant "Alleluia!" sung in response to the word of forgiveness. Sing with joy and enthusiasm, with full band accompaniment including lots of percussion. Emphasize the back beat (2 and 4) rather than 1 and 3. If you wish, make use of the quieter stanzas sung over the hummed refrain. The stanzas fit the baptism theme perfectly, though they cause the song to be sung with a bit more restraint.

Out of the silence at the end of the last song, the drums begin the song "Praise to the Lord, the Almighty" (PsH 253, Key of F) with a distinctive and memorable pattern:

The figure is repeated twice, then the piano and violin play the last line as an introduction. The figure is repeated twice again before the congregation begins singing. It is then repeated after each musical phrase (which adds one extra bar per phrase). On the fourth stanza, it is sung accompanied only by drums, which drop out altogether on "let the amen" and come in again on "again."

Liturgical Notes: Leader says, "Let the amen sound from his people again!" **(Amen!)** "Amen?" **(Amen.)**

Then make a transition either into baptism or into the prayer for illumination (below).

INITIATION (BAPTISM)

Liturgical Notes: If you are celebrating baptism, insert the liturgy here. It should include, minimally, the words of institution from Matthew 28, a prayer of thanksgiving, promises made by the parents and congregation, baptism in the name of the Father, Son, and Holy Spirit, a prayer of intercession for the one baptized and for the world, and a closing song. It may also include a creed, renunciation of evil, a blessing, and a welcome to the new member.

If no baptism is planned, consider having the congregation renew their baptismal vows. A service for doing so can be found in *Sing! A New Creation* (240).

PREPARATION/ILLUMINATION

Liturgical Notes: Leader says something like the following: "Lord God, Holy Spirit, open our eyes now to your presence among us—in the water and in your Word. Speak to us exactly what we each need to hear. We pray in Jesus' name. Amen."

Musical Notes: "Thy Word" (SNC 86). Key of E♭. Create a quiet arrangement of this Michael W. Smith/Amy Grant favorite that emphasizes not the intercessory or declarative mode of the stanzas, but rather the anticipatory mood of the chorus. Asking, pleading for light. For example, play moderato (66 bpm). The right hand of the piano plays up one register while the guitar strums an arpeggio once per measure on the downbeat.

PROCLAMATION

Liturgical Notes: Scripture: Romans 1:1-7

Notes on Scripture reading:

- To give Scripture its due weight, bookend the reading with a significant chunk (five seconds) of silence.
- Paul is notoriously difficult to comprehend when read aloud, so the slower it is read, the better.

Outline:

Called to Belong to Jesus Christ
Foundation: "Through [Christ] and for his name's sake we have received grace. . . ."
   —expressed in our baptisms

Purpose: "Called to belong to Jesus Christ . . ."
   —to be with him
   —to become like him
   —to be for him
   amid my own life's circumstances.
Outcome: Called Daily
   —to live in and with Jesus Christ
   —to be the Good News to others

DEDICATION

Musical Notes: After a surfeit of words, sing something straightforward, simple, meditative—"Lord, I Want to Be a Christian" (SFL 40). Key of D. With this song, the lyrics can be changed to adjust to particular color of the sermon. Accompany very simply, prayerfully. First piano, then guitar and bass and strings take over. A cappella if the congregation is strong enough. If not, go straight into next song without transition (just an introduction).

Sing "Holiness/Take My Life" (MSPW 91) with gentle intensity. Key of G. Strings or other instruments capable of sustained tones fill in the harmonies. After singing all the way through, the band can continue playing as an offering is either taken or brought forward.

Liturgical Notes: The leader invites the congregation to respond with their offerings.

Musical Notes: After the offering, sing "Holiness/Take My Life" again, either the refrain alone, or the refrain and a stanza. End a cappella.

Liturgical Notes: The leader says, "Lord, you have named us, called us, put your sign on us, saved us. We respond to you by giving you all our lives. We pray that you will transform us to be more and more like Jesus, with his love, his holiness, his faithfulness, his righteousness animating us. Send us now into the world you love so much. May we follow you every day of our lives. In Christ's name we pray. Amen."

Musical Notes: "Cry of My Heart" (SNC 81). Key of D. An upbeat song of dedication, praying for Christ to "teach . . . your holy ways" and "make me wholly devoted to you." Avoid imitations of recordings that insert superfluous a "ooh—ooh—ooh" between stanza and chorus; avoid also "clever" arrangements. The song's syncopation makes it bright and infectious. No need to strain to energize a congregation.

Conclude and go straight to next song, playing introduction underneath pastor's blessing.

BENEDICTION

Liturgical Notes: Leader says, "Listen to these words from Saint Paul: 'Whatever you do, in word or deed, do everything in the name of the Lord Jesus, giving thanks to God the Father through him' (Col. 3:17).

"Now, as we leave, you are to be priests to one another, giving each other this blessing, and giving God the glory."

Musical Notes: "Benediction/My Friends, May You Grow in Grace" (SNC 288). Key of D. The music reflects the distinction in the text between the first and second parts. The first section is in a lower vocal range than second. Sing twice. The first part more quietly, with the congregation's members looking at each other. Sing the second half with more exultation, breaking into harmony, clasping hands and raising arms and eyes heavenward.

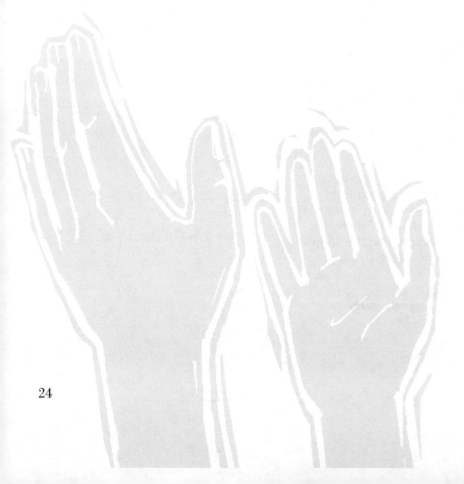

For All the Saints

Hebrews 12:1-3

All Saints, traditionally celebrated on November 1 or the Sunday after, is a feast day not often observed by Protestant Christians for at least two reasons. First, ever since the Reformation, we have lingering suspicions about saints. In the church's history, saints have evoked subtle (or rank) idolatry, and we Protestants are eager to steer clear of every temptation we can identify. This is so, even though *saint* is an innocuous—even scriptural—term for all those who follow Jesus as faithfully as they are able. Saints are merely those whose progress in holiness is expanded by their openness to the Holy Spirit. The second reason we know little of saints is that at the end of October, we children of the Reformation choose to celebrate Reformation Day instead of All Saints Day (if "celebrate" is the correct word for a necessary but painful schism in the Body of Christ).

In the past, this alteration in our ecclesial calendar may have been a prudent choice; but over the centuries it has left us, in my opinion, impoverished. Compared to our Roman Catholic and Orthodox sisters and brothers, we have a diminished sense of the church's universality in both time and place. This worship service is an attempt to address this deficiency. It is an attempt to worship God with awareness of the "great cloud of witnesses" with whom we do so week in and week out.

Typically the church remembers the saints on All Saint's Day with a long prayer that includes three things:

- Thanksgiving for our heritage of faith, for the saints who modeled faith in Christ and who preserved it in years past.
- Remembrance of local saints who were translated into glory in the preceding twelve months.
- Intercession for the world church and all its millions of living saints.

In this service these three parts are spread throughout the service. The thanksgiving takes place near the beginning of worship, the intercession near the middle, and the memorial as part of the text of the sermon.

The remembrance of and connection to the worldwide church is accomplished in two ways. First and most important are the musical choices. The congregation sings songs from nearly every continent, songs that originate in the fourth century, the fourteenth, the twentieth—and a few in between. Making a service like this worshipful requires a strong worship leadership team and an adventurous congregation (and a patient one, as the service clocks in at over ninety minutes). It also takes lots of preparation. Do not be content to project lyrics only for the congregation; print out all the music, with explanatory notes, if necessary.

The second connection with the world church is made with spoken words. Since most of the world songs chosen in this service are simple and easy to learn—even on one hearing—they gain depth and richness from the prayers, Scripture, and liturgical context in which they're placed.

CONGREGATION

Musical Notes: Before the service begins, have a leader teach the first song, "Come, All You People" (SNC 4) to the congregation. Key of E. Teach all four parts, and learn it from memory so no books or projection are needed. When everyone knows it, begin the spoken psalm (if desired, over a very faint percussive persistence).

Liturgical Notes: Leader begins with words from Psalm 100 (the words may also be projected). They may be read responsively between leader and congregation, or between two leaders as follows:

Make a joyful noise to the LORD, all the earth!
Worship the LORD with gladness;
come into his presence with singing.
Know that the LORD is God.
It is he that made us, and we are his;
we are his people and the sheep of his pasture.
Enter his gates with thanksgiving, and his courts with praise.
Give thanks to him, bless his name.
For the LORD is good; his steadfast love endures forever,
and his faithfulness to all generations.

Musical Notes: Now sing "Come, All You People." Initiate this infectious call to worship with lots of percussion, strong four-part singing, and as few tonal instruments as possible (none is best). A djembe or other "booming" drum should play a steady and heavy downbeat, helping the congregation step and sway; grounding the song into the earth God made rather than letting it sail off into the sky.

CELEBRATION

Musical Notes: The percussion immediately begins the next song of praise, "Sing of the Lord's Goodness" (GC 547). Key of Em. This memorable song, in both rhythm and chord structure, is a 5/4 take-off on the Dave Brubeck jazz classic "Take Five." Though a good pianist can accompany alone, for congregational support it's best to have a full rhythm section, including trap set. There's no substitute for listening to a recording, but if players aren't familiar with "Take Five," the shortcut to the right "feel" is a heavy accent on beats 1, 4, and 5. Make sure a single solo instrument—a sax is best—plays the melody with strength to lead the congregation. The temptation will be to play too fast with too much intensity. But this is jazz, a relaxed celebration of God's goodness. Play slowly enough so the congregation can wrap their tongues around the rich text from Psalm 98. Feel free to repeat the chorus twice after the last stanza.

APPRECIATION

Liturgical Notes: Leader prays as follows: "Lord God, we bless your name. We bring you our songs of praise and thanks for all you do, for all you are. You call your children from every nation and from every time. We give thanks for our brothers and sisters in Africa, in Asia, in Latin America, and for the gifts they give us: courage in the face of persecution, excitement about life in the Spirit, songs that expand our horizons and enlarge our vision of your big world and your great love.

"We give thanks for our mothers and fathers in faith, grandparents and heroes and all the saints who have gone before us, following you wherever you called them. We thank you for what they taught, what they prayed, how they lived. May we too finish the race strong, our eyes fixed on your Son, Jesus Christ, whose name we lift up and praise and exalt."

Leader may wish to conclude the prayer with the prayer of a saint, like this one from the third-century Syrian Orthodox tradition:

"O most glorious and exalted Lord, you are glorified in the heights above by ministers of fire and spirit . . . yet in your love you wish to be glorified by humans on earth as well. . . . Free us, Lord, in your compassion, from whatever cares hinder the worship of you, and teach us to seek the kingdom and its righteousness. . . . May we become worthy of that kingdom along with the saints who have done your will, and may we sing your praises."

—Maronite Shehimto, from *Oxford Book of Prayer,*
© 1985 Oxford University Press.

ADORATION

Musical Notes: "He Is Exalted" (SNC 41). Key of F. This song and the next may be played ½ step down in the key of E if you wish to make seamless transitions. To allow the praise to grow in this song and the next, begin this familiar number with a thinner accompaniment—perhaps just the piano and some light percussion. Sing twice, broadening in tempo at the end to a comfortable pace to sing "Holy God, We Praise Your Name" (PsH 504). Key of F (or E). Play the introduction softly underneath the reading of Scripture (below).

Liturgical Notes: Leader reads Revelation 7:9-10:

9 After this I looked, and there was a great multitude that no one could count, from every nation, from all tribes and peoples and languages, standing before the throne and before the Lamb, robed in white, with palm branches in their hands. **10** They cried out in a loud voice, saying, "Salvation belongs to our God who is seated on the throne, and to the Lamb!"

Musical Notes: When the reading is finished, play the song's last line to cue the congregation. Then accompany this ancient prayer with strength and wonder. The goal is a glimpse of heavenly worship. Broaden as the third stanza begins, and then sing a cappella, starting in unison and adding a new voice at each phrase. Have the organ join in on the last stanza, encourage sopranos to sing the descant (double it on a flute or violin), and make judicious use of cymbal swells to convey awe and power.

Then, as leader begins prayer, the organ or synth or piano can gently ease into the "Kyrie" (below), played in four simple parts.

Liturgical Notes: Leader prays as follows: "Triune God, mystery beyond all understanding, today we join the saints and angels and all creation exalting you and giving you honor and glory. Salvation belongs to you. And power and might and holiness. When we see your holiness, we tremble with fear and with awe, with love and attraction. We wish to be like you, to be near you, to stand forever in your presence."

CONFESSION/LAMENTATION

Liturgical Notes: Leader continues, praying as follows: "But we know we cannot. We are spoiled by sin, by pride and greed and envy and sloth, by lust and gluttony and anger. By all that infects us and infests the world you gave us to care for. In your mercy pour out your salvation upon us."

Musical Notes: "Kyrie Eleison" (SNC 52). Key of E. Sing quietly, reverently, two times through. The music may continue underneath the prayer *without* playing a discernable melody.

INTERCESSION

Musical Notes: Play the B7 chord to cue the congregation to sing the "Kyrie" again after each of the prayer's three sections (below).

Or you may choose to have silence in between the sections of prayer and then conclude all the prayers with the "Kyrie" or the beautiful Korean prayer "Ososo" (SNC 209). Key of Gm. Play simply, accompanied by piano, flute, and triangle or hand cymbals on beat 1.

Liturgical Notes: Leader continues prayer as follows: "We think of *(mention congregational concerns)*. Lord, have mercy.

"We think of *(mention local and national concerns)*. Lord, have mercy.

"We think of *(mention world concerns, especially those of the worldwide church)*. Lord, have mercy."

The liturgist/leader may then conclude with a summarizing prayer.

REDEMPTION

Liturgical Notes: Leader says something like the following: "Our worship is a taste of heaven—a glimpse of the glory that awaits us. When God gave Moses, hiding in the rock, a glimpse of only the backside of this glory, the Bible tells us that Moses saw this:

*6*The LORD, the LORD, a God merciful and gracious, slow to anger, and abounding in steadfast love and faithfulness, *7* keeping steadfast love for the thousandth generation, forgiving iniquity and transgression and sin (Ex. 34:6-7a).

"Dear friends, the good news of the gospel is this: Our God loves us, and in Jesus Christ, we are forgiven. Amen!"

DECLARATION/PROFESSION

Liturgical Notes: Leader continues: "All that we believe as Christians centers in this forgiveness, in God's gift of Jesus and his presence with us in the Spirit. And every Christian saint, in every time and place—both extraordinary ones and garden-variety saints like you and me—each one has professed one Lord, one faith, one baptism. Let's together speak and sing the faith that makes us one:

[Project the words for Apostles' Creed.]

Musical Notes: As creed ends, begin introduction to the song of unity, "Somos uno en Cristo" (SNC 179). Key of Em. Accompany with guitars and strings. Sing in unison, with firmness, but don't let it plod. To prevent that, use percussion to create this lilting rhythmic figure:

DEDICATION

Liturgical Notes: The offering may either be collected or brought forward by members of the congregation. A service like this is a wonderful opportunity to take an offering to assist in hunger relief or other worldwide efforts to point to God's kingdom of shalom. (At LOFT, we took up a collection for international students. We bought them phone cards so they could connect with the families back home they missed so much). The leader could highlight the offering as an act of worship to God and oneness with our brothers and sisters in Christ around the world.

Musical Notes: Instrumental music—choose a song that can move with ease into a bright doxology. After the offering sing "Praise God from Whom All Blessings Flow" (PsH 637). Key of C. This gospel-flavored doxology is a challenge to do well with a band. Let the piano lead and sing boldly.

PREPARATION

Liturgical Notes: Leader offers prayer of illumination, perhaps the prayer of a saint, like this sixth-century one from Saint Benedict of Nursia: "O Gracious and Holy God, give us diligence to seek you, wisdom to perceive you, and patience to wait for you. Grant us, O God, a mind to meditate on you, eyes to behold you; ears to listen for your Word; a heart to love you; and a life to proclaim you; through the power of the Spirit of Jesus Christ our Lord. Amen."

Musical Notes: "Come, Holy Spirit" (SNC 165). Key of B♭. This simple echo song should be sung without any accompaniment. Sing back and forth between two congregational halves or between leader and people. The song ends off tonic, with a tone of expectancy and anticipation of the Word about to be proclaimed.

PROCLAMATION

Scripture: Hebrews 12:1-3

Outline:

Introduction: Portraits on walls of hallowed institution. Surrounded by cloud of witnesses.

1. Looking at these saints, do we feel
   —encouraged?
   —intimidated? The world was not worthy of them. What about me?
   —tired? The sin that entangles.
2. Perhaps we ought to look not at saints, but at Jesus, author and perfecter of our faith. We're not in to win, but to play. Like the Special Olympics.
3. Crowd noise
   —whooping and hollering encouragement
   —pointing to Jesus, who helped when another step was impossible
4. The finish line
   —Revelation 7: picture of saints at worship
   —Faces you recognize? Paul, Peter, Aquinas, Martin Luther, Martin Luther King, Mother Teresa . . .
   —members of congregation who died recently
   —practicing "perfect praise"—our destiny

ADORATION

Musical Notes: "For All the Saints" (PsH 505). Key of G. This song builds on the sermon's conclusion, pointing to our worshiping destiny in heaven and the saints already there. The song wants to go to heaven, so don't start in the stratosphere; begin where we are—with a humble piano, and maybe a light snare drum, especially in the second and third stanzas (the military ones). Build gently into the fourth and fifth stanzas, which should be sung quieter, in SATB rather than in unison. On the words "distant triumph song," bring in the organ on a single stop in a high register. Gradually fill in until organ is the dominant instrument at the "alleluias." Then crescendo gradually through the last two stanzas until the very end.

DEDICATION

Liturgical Notes: Leader prays as follows: "Holy and Mighty God—Father, Son, and Holy Spirit—we praise you for your glory, for keeping your people throughout the ages, and for creating a destiny for us with so much splendor. May we remember with joy those who have finished the race. May we be encouraged by their example. And with our eyes fixed on you, may we live lives worthy of the love you have shown them and us. May we become someday like those saints, singing, praising, waving palm branches, honoring you, marching around your throne, giving you glory. Lord, we want to be in that number, when your saints come marching in."

Musical Notes: "When the Saints Go Marching In" (TFF 180). Key of D. Sing exuberant song of praise and hope with as much energy as you can. If you have the musical horses, a Dixieland treatment with trombone and clarinet is ideal. However you accompany, make sure the tempo is brisk and clap on beats 2 and 4.

BENEDICTION

Liturgical Notes: Leader says, "Hear God's blessing: The Lord watch over your going out and your coming in, from this time forth, and forever more. Amen.

"In heaven, the saints march in. But here on earth, they march *out* too—out of this place and into the world Jesus gave his life for. We march out to witness to Jesus. We march out to be his hands and feet, bringing food and clothing and care. We march out to work for justice and peace. We march out in the light of God."

RECESSION

Musical Notes: "Siyahamba" (SNC 293). Key of G. As with the opening song, let percussion take the central role here, along with the voices. Involve as many people as possible. Hand out everything in your box of what I affectionately call "shukka-shukkas"—hand percussion (a djembe or congas, a guiro, a shaker, claves, and so on). A bass or piano gives the pitch and then allows the congregation to sing with verve and spirit. They harmonize as they are able. Alternate singing in Zulu, English, and Spanish. The song has ebb and flow as it dips and rises in intensity and volume. The leader may shout out additional stanzas (marching, praying, shouting). The song ends suddenly, without a ritard.

Singing the Church Year

Matthew 28:1-6

Unlike other LOFT services, which take place on Sunday night and go for seventy-five minutes or more, this hymn sing service took place on a Friday and lasted under twenty-five minutes. It was part of a week-long project of educating students about the seasons of the church and what it means to find our identity, as Paul says, *in Christ,* inserting our stories into his story, giving our own lives context and purpose.

CONGREGATION

Musical Notes: The music begins immediately, even a few minutes before "official" start time.

ADORATION

Musical Notes: "O Come, Let Us Adore Him" (SPW 248). Key of F (one step lower than written music). To encourage the congregation to enter more deeply into adoration as they sing, introduce with just the piano. Other instruments are added each stanza (four in all): violin, bass, guitars playing arpeggios, and cymbal swells from the drummer. Build in intensity and volume until end. Repeat first stanza, this time a cappella.

Liturgical Notes: After song concludes, leader says something like the following: "The Lord be with you. **(And also with you.)** Welcome to _____. Today we are going to conclude our week-long series on the seasons and feasts of the church by journeying through the church year in song."

LAMENTATION

Liturgical Notes: Leader continues, "Our journey begins in Advent where we find the Israelites—and ourselves—in 'lonely exile' awaiting Christ's coming. But we sing with hope too (rejoice!), because of God's sure promises. Please join us."

Musical Notes: "O Come, O Come, Immanuel" (PsH 328, st. 1, 6). Play in Fm (half step up from written music) to make transition easier. Get at the song's loneliness with a spare accompaniment on the stanzas (solo cello, guitar, and flute), and at the song's hope with a two-handed keyboard joining on refrain. Let the first "rejoice!" sing out, and the next be a softer echo.

As the song concludes, piano transitions back into F major. Gentle introduction of the refrain of "Go, Tell It on the Mountain."

CELEBRATION

Liturgical Notes: While piano introduces "Go, Tell It on the Mountain," leader says, "Our Advent hope is rewarded at Christmas, when we hear of the birth of our Savior. We burst with joy, and our joy spills over into Epiphany and into the whole world as we encourage one another to tell everyone the good news that Jesus Christ is born."

Musical Notes: "Go Tell It on the Mountain" (PsH 356). Key of F. Vocalists should cue congregational participation beginning not with the refrain, but with stanza 1: "While shepherds . . ." Play quietly, slowly, *rubato*—with anticipation. Use just the piano, one chord per bar, making use of the higher registers. Hold the last chord of the stanza as long as possible, then snap off. *A tempo* (briskly), walk the bass up to F, and let the whole band join in celebrating, swinging. A saxophone or other brass can take it up another notch.

CONFESSION

Liturgical Notes: After singing, leader prays along these lines: "Christ Jesus, we give you thanks for coming to dwell among us, to teach us how to live and how to love. We confess that as we try to follow your example, we often mess up. You urge us to holiness, but our hearts are fouled with our own sin *(add specific confessions).* Forgive us, Lord. *(Do not end prayer with "Amen" or "in Jesus' name" but let the prayer continue with the song.)*

Musical Notes: Near end of prayer, begin introduction to "Create in Me" (SNC 49). Key of G. Keep the accompaniment spare and prayerful. Introduce with the last line played by a plaintive violin and guitar. Piano and bass join when congregation begins singing. Sing twice through.

REDEMPTION

Liturgical Notes: Leader says something like this: "During Lent, we remember our sinfulness, we ask for forgiveness, and as we follow Jesus into the last week of his life, we contemplate with awe the mystery of his sacrifice for our sakes."

Musical Notes: "What Wondrous Love Is This" (PsH 379, st. 1-2). Key of Dm. Single instrument introduction. To worship as thoughtfully as possible, sing a cappella.

PROCLAMATION

Liturgical Notes: When music concludes, observe a moment of silence. Then, without further explanation, leader reads—or better yet, tells from memory—Matthew 28:1-6, the story of the resurrection.

CELEBRATION

Musical Notes: Drums, piano, and violin begin the celebratory "Celtic Alleluia" (SNC 148) immediately as Scripture reading ends. Key of G (one step below written music). For a very Celtic feel, a low tom drum (mimicking a bhodran) begins with a quarter-eighth pattern. The violin plays a *sfz*-attacked two-string drone on G and D (two beats/measure, no chord changes). The piano simply plays G in octaves down low. A tin whistle or soprano recorder plays the melody all the way through the refrain once. Then the congregation joins in. Hard snare rim shots on the three beats of the half-measure before the stanza begins give the congregation a clear cue where to begin. Piano joins providing melody and harmonic support on the stanzas, the drone harmony returns on the refrain. The penny whistle can go to the descant on the refrain when the congregation is confident in their singing.

The song concludes with two measures of the percussive drum and violin drone, a slight ritard, the last notes ringing out.

INTERCESSION

Liturgical Notes: Leader says something like this: "Our risen Lord ascends to heaven, but does not leave us alone—on the feast of Pentecost he sends us the Holy Spirit to comfort, to inspire, to unite, to renew us and the whole earth.

"Sing and learn with us this new song, a fresh breath of the Spirit. The stanzas will be sung for you, but please join on the refrain. Don't worry if we have trouble, and our music sounds like little more than people mumbling in many languages—that might be fitting. Please join us."

Musical Notes: Sing "Send Us Your Spirit" (SNC 163). Key of D. Sing gently, steadily, prayerfully. Soloists may sing the stanzas from various locations within the congregation. First stanza accompanied by piano, second by guitar, third by both. When the congregation sings the refrain after the stanzas 2 and 3, have a solo instrument play the melody a measure behind, in canon.

DEDICATION

Liturgical Notes: Leader prays as follows: "Holy Spirit, renewed daily by your love, may we follow Jesus through the rest of this day, this month, this whole year. Fill our days, our average, ordinary days with love for you, with humility and purpose for ourselves, and with compassion for our world. When we fall down, pick us up. Encourage us with your grace. May we do all that you have called us to, filled only with Jesus Christ, our All in All."

ADORATION

Musical Notes: "You Are My All in All" (SPW 220). Key of G. To fill the room with adoration, accompany with full band and sing with gusto one time through together, then in canon another time and a half. A piano introduction with a guitar playing in thirds (à la Van Morrison's classic songs) gives this the right feel.

BENEDICTION

Liturgical Notes: Leader offers a benediction: "People of God, hear God's blessing: The grace of the Lord Jesus Christ, the love of God, and the communion of the Holy Spirit be with all of you" (2 Cor. 13:13).

RECESSION

Liturgical Notes: Leader dismisses the congregation: "Go now into this season of light, marching together in the peace and the light of God. You may leave as we sing." (At the LOFT, we held this service during Epiphany.)

Musical Notes: "Siyahamba" (SNC 293). Use as much percussion as you can—especially hand percussion—but let the celebration be grounded, not flighty. Have a bass or piano give the pitch, and then allow the congregation to sing with verve and spirit, harmonizing as they are able.

Advent: A Time to Be Silent

Ecclesiastes 3:1, 7b

Most worshiping communities struggle a little with the season of Advent. The undertow of Christmas is so strong that it's hard not to get sucked into the celebratory frenzy beforehand. It's hard to keep those December weeks a season of waiting, of hope, of anticipation. The following, then, is an attempt to walk a line between Advent and Christmas.

The service's theme is silence: silence as part of the rhythm of life since creation (Gen. 1); as part of the wisdom of the world (Eccl. 3); and as the context of the Incarnation (John 1). In the fullness of time, at last, God speaks the Word into the world.

One of the challenges is to create an environment where silences can be as lively and participatory as the rest of the service. This service tries to create that environment in four ways. First, it speaks, in Scripture, sermon, and song, about the importance of silence. Second, it carves out three significant spots for the congregation to rest in worshipful silence. Third, it employs a "declamatory decrescendo"—a gradual diminishing of verbiage from the outset of the service to the end. Fourth, many of the songs are chant-based, the simplest and purest form of sung words.

Throughout the service all liturgists, leaders, prayers, and readers should be at ease with calm moments, with longish pauses between songs, and with big stillness both before and after each Scripture reading. They should strive to create a sense of being comfortable with the silence in which God's Word is spoken and heard.

CONGREGATION

Liturgical Notes: Leader begins by reading (from memory, if possible) Jeremiah 33:2-3:

2 Thus says the LORD who made the earth, the LORD who formed it to establish it—the LORD is his name: *3* Call to me and I will answer you, and will tell you great and hidden things that you have not known.

Leader then continues as follows: "'Call to me,' says the Lord, 'and I will answer you.' Let's together call upon the Lord.

"Lord, you are worthy to be praised. We love you, we worship you. And we pray that in the next hour, you will reveal to us the great and hidden things we each need to know. Speak to our hearts from yours. We pray in Jesus' name, amen."

37

Musical Notes: While the leader speaks, the band—or just one guitar—may begin an introductory vamp for the first song. But it is perhaps just as effective to be silent.

After the reading, sing "I Will Call Upon the Lord" (SPW 224). Key of D. Accompany this echo song primarily with guitars. So that it has a slightly anticipatory character, sing a bit more slowly than usual (72 bpm). Sing twice through (no more), then go straight into the introduction, starting at the "Aleluya," for the next song.

CELEBRATION

Musical Notes: "Cantemos al Señor" (SNC 40). Key of Dm. This is a song of praise to God the Creator. Sing at the pace of stanza 2's "hopeful waiting"—no faster than the last song (dotted quarter = 72 bpm). This leaves room for some creative percussive ornamentation and allows Anglo congregations to try singing in Spanish. Again, guitars should lead the accompaniment. Build into the last "Aleluya!"

ADORATION

Liturgical Notes: The leader says something like the following: "Lord of grace and beauty, we join with the sky and sea and sun and stars that you made, and we praise you. You are grand and glorious. You are mighty and holy. As we come before you now, still us and speak to us in your silence. Amen.

"Let's together sing 'Be Still,' and then let us be still, listening in silence for the Word of the Lord."

Musical Notes: As leader finishes speaking, the band quietly begins an introduction to "Be Still, for the Presence" (SNC 11). Key of D. Sing with reverent stillness, creating "holy ground" with the music. Be careful—too many cymbal swells and synth stacks and the holy ground becomes a syrupy swamp. Don't fill the sonic space with instrumental accompaniment. Play as sparingly as possible.

Liturgical Notes: *[Observe a time of silence—at least two minutes, ideally more.]*

Then leader reads, slowly and deliberately, Genesis 1:1-5:

1 In the beginning when God created the heavens and the earth, *2* the earth was a formless void and darkness covered the face of the deep, while a wind from God swept over the face of the waters. *3* Then God said, "Let there be light"; and there was light. *4* And God saw that the light was good; and God separated the light from the darkness. *5* God called the light Day, and the darkness he called Night. And there was evening and there was morning, the first day.

After a suitable pause, the leader says, "God spoke, and it was. God is a God of wonders. Let's offer him our lives, our gifts, our praise."

The offering is taken.

Musical Notes: As the offering is taken, the congregation sings (or has sung for them) a psalmic song of praise: "God of Wonders" (MSPW2 80). Key of G. (Note that this song lends itself to a simply put-together PowerPoint presentation of the creation images to which the lyrics point.) Begin gently, quietly. A single voice and a single guitar. The first refrain is still subdued. Then build as you go, adding hand percussion, bass, piano, electric guitar, synth, violin, and so on. The song reaches its zenith of praise at the second refrain and bridge. Return to the chorus one time and drop all instruments. The next time, bring the band back in. For a subtle touch, have a violin repeat the first line from the hymn "Holy Holy Holy" (NICAEA) at the words "you are holy."

CONFESSION

Out of the comfortable silence at the song's diminuendo conclusion, the leader reads Malachi 3:1-3 (the Scripture may be projected as well):

1b The Lord whom you seek will suddenly come to his temple. . . . *2* But who can endure the day of his coming, and who can stand when he appears? For he is like a refiner's fire . . . *3* he will sit as a refiner and purifier of silver, and he will purify the descendants of Levi and refine them like gold and silver, until they present offerings to the LORD in righteousness.

Then the leader says, "Let us pray: Holy God, you know our hearts, and you know how fouled up they are with sin. *(May present more specific prayers of confession.)* Forgive us. Heal us. Purify us."

[Conclude with a time of silent prayer.]

Musical Notes: As this prayer concludes, the piano gives the introduction to "Purify My Heart" (MSPW2 90). Key of D. The rhythm section should offer minimal support, but enough to carry the congregation through long phrases and notes held for 6 counts. For a slightly more penitential character, alter the chords for the penultimate "purify my heart" to read G, F#7, Bm7, Bm7/A. Take a tiny breath, and sing the last line with a small ritard. Have one instrument (piano or guitar or even organ) make a transition into the next song as follows: Ending on D, play a C in the bass, then a Bsus, then hold on B, get the tempo, and begin, in Em.

INTERCESSION

Liturgical Notes: Leader prays as follows: "Lord, purify our hearts. Purify our lives, our church, our whole world. As we sing, we offer you all those prayers for which we have words and those for which we have no words—and those we don't even know enough to pray. Hear us, O Lord, and answer us."

Musical Notes: "O Lord, Hear My Prayer" (SNC 204). Key of Em. This song from the ecumenical Community of Taizé is conducive to meditative prayer. Sing slowly and expressively in four strong parts. Repeat between five and ten times through. Keep a constant keyboard or piano, while solo instruments (violin, clarinet, flutes or recorders) play descants that give the song texture and depth. As the song ends, hold the Em chord, and have a single orchestral instrument, preferably one with a somber timbre, play an introduction to the next song: "O Come, O Come, Immanuel" (PsH 328). Key of Em. Stanzas 1 and 2 or 1 and 7. Play plaintively, one voice and instrument on melody, and one instrument on the bass line. Keep the meter fairly strict, lest it become croony. Add a full four-part keyboard on the refrain. Let the first "rejoice!" sing out, and the next be a softer echo.

PREPARATION

Liturgical Notes: Leader prays as follows: "Come, Immanuel, God with us. By your Holy Spirit, open our ears, and minds and hearts. Amen."

PROCLAMATION

Scripture: Ecclesiastes 3: 1, 7b.

Outline:

A Time to Be Silent
Introduction: Silence puzzles people.
1. The loss of silence in the world today.
2. Silence is part of the rhythm of life.
3. The wise know when to speak, when to be silent.
4. God
    —Silence (Advent)
    —Word (Christmas)

[Follow the sermon with an unannounced, extended period of silence (at least four minutes).]

Musical Notes: Out of the silence, a lone instrument (again, with a plaintive, somber tone, and in straight meter), plays once through "Let All Mortal Flesh Keep Silence" (PsH 341). Key of Dm. Sing stanzas 1, 3, and 4, adding instruments and voices to an exultant climax in the last words: "Alleluia, Lord Most High!"

Liturgical Notes: [*Observe another period of extended silence.*]

Then leader, unannounced, slowly and meaningfully reads the gospel lesson (John 1, 1-4, 14):

1 In the beginning was the Word, and the Word was with God, and the Word was God. *2* He was in the beginning with God. *3* All things came into being through him, and without him not one thing came into being. What has come into being *4* in him was life, and the life was the light of all people. *14* The Word became flesh and lived among us, and we have seen his glory, the glory as of a father's only son, full of grace and truth.

Musical Notes: A solo instrument—this time with a warm tone and in free meter—introduces "Of the Father's Love Begotten" (PsH 342). Key of D (half step down from written music). Play the last half as introduction. Then a keyboard and the vocalists should lead the congregation with strength, pausing to breathe at each phrase. As the last chord (D) echoes, add the 7th, and then change to a G as a guitar begins strumming, in 6/8, an introduction to the next song.

DEDICATION

Musical Notes: "Awake, Awake and Greet the New Morn" (SNC 91). Key of G. Sing this bright song of fulfillment with joy, even boisterously. Accompany with guitar, tambourine, woodwinds, piano.

BENEDICTION

Liturgical Notes: Leader offers a blessing based on Luke 2: "Lord, now dismiss your servants in peace, according to your word; for we have seen your salvation, which you have prepared in the presence of all peoples, a light for revelation to the Gentiles and for glory to your people Israel. Go in peace to love and serve the Lord."

The poem "Word" by Madeleine L'Engle may be printed in the bulletin (with permission from the publisher):

I, who live by words, am wordless when
I try my words in prayer. All language turns
To silence. Prayer will take my words and then
Reveal their emptiness. The stilled voice learns
To hold its peace, to listen with the heart
To silence that is joy, is adoration.
The self is shattered, all words torn apart
In this strange patterned time of contemplation
That, in time, breaks time, breaks words, breaks me,
And then, in silence, leaves me healed and mended.
I leave, returned to language, for I see
Through words, even when all words are ended.
I, who live by words, am wordless when
I turn me to the Word to pray. Amen.

Epiphany: Luminescence
Philippians 2:12-18

Light—beheld in a dazzling star, hidden under a bushel, reflected in a human face. In all its forms, light is one of the richest and most prominent of all Christian images. From the stirring fiat "Let there be light" in the opening chapters of Genesis to Jesus Christ, whose presence illumines Revelation's everlasting city, the whole of Scripture seems lit up from within. The emphasis isn't so much on us who shine, but on God who shines.

This is true even in exhortatory passages like the one from Philippians that makes up the heart of this service. Though it speaks of our shining "as stars in a dark world," it is plain that whatever luminescence we possess is borrowed from the Light of the world. This service plan tries to reflect this truth as we sing first about the light of Christ and end by dedicating ourselves to letting our own light shine.

A service like this suggests an opportunity to do something with actual light. Specific suggestions are not offered in this plan, since lighting is so dependent upon natural light, time of day, availability of artificial light resources, and so on. Do think creatively about how to alter or manipulate the light in your worship space so that what you do points to the Light of the world and to our own light.

CONGREGATION

Liturgical Notes: The service begins as the leader says, "Long ago, the prophet Isaiah spoke to the people of Israel words that God now speaks to us: Arise, shine, for your light has come, and the glory of the Lord has risen upon you. Nations shall come to your light, and kings to the brightness of your dawn (Isa. 60:1, 3).

"People of God, arise! Shine! Sing! For now is the time to worship!"

While the leader is speaking, the band softly plays an introduction to the opening song.

Musical Notes: "Come, Now Is the Time to Worship" (MSPW2 56). Key of D. A muted right-hand strum on an acoustic guitar provides the rhythms that drive this song, a persistent invitation to worship. A synth can provide sustained chords underneath during the subdued first section, and then let everyone loose at "One day every tongue will confess." Bring it back to a quiet intensity as you repeatedly sing the concluding request: "come."

ADORATION

Liturgical Notes: Leader prays as follows: "Everlasting God of light, before your presence angels veil their faces. But you show us the brightness of your love in your Son, Jesus. We pray that you will show yourself to all nations and fill the world with your glory; though him who is the true Light and the bright morning star, Jesus Christ. In his name we pray. Amen."

Musical Notes: Silence during the reading is appropriate. But if you wish a transition from D, have the guitar play a Bm7, then A. Go back and forth between those two chords under the prayer. Come out of the prayer with Bm7, E7sus, E7, and then into the introduction to "Shine, Jesus, Shine" (SNC 128). Key of A. This contagious contemporary hymn should be sung with liveliness. Clap your hands, enjoy the syncopation, sing as an enthusiastic prayer.

If this song is too familiar to your congregation, another good possibility is the Michael W. Smith song "Shine on Us" (MSPW 19). Key of D, one step up from written music. Also an enthusiastic prayer, play brightly with a steady, driving bass. Subdivide the accompaniment to support the long held notes of the melody.

If you prefer seamless transitions, hold the A final chord (A), add the seventh, and then move on, playing the next few songs in the key of D (half step from written music). But it's also fine to let the last tones of the A chord ring on the guitar and then have the keyboard initiate the last line of the next song — "Beautiful Savior" (PsH 461) in the more distant key of E♭. Sing this beloved favorite with full-throated adoration. Let stanza 2 go unaccompanied, and then gradually add instruments (no percussion except cymbal swells) through stanza 3. Broaden the tempo slightly in the fourth.

CONFESSION

Musical Notes: Without slowing down, play the refrain once through for the song of confession, "Shine on Me" (SNC 51). Key of E♭. Though it has a pleading tone, sing this prayer—especially the refrain—with confidence in God's mercy. Sing the refrain, stanza 1, refrain, stanza 2, and the refrain again. Band continues playing the stanza underneath the spoken prayer.

Liturgical Notes: Before the last measure of the refrain for stanza 2 ends, leader begins praying aloud as follows: "Almighty God, you sent Jesus among us to be light of the world. But we confess that because of our sin we don't often reflect that light—sometimes we don't even see it. We are dim reflections in this dark world, where we ought to shine like stars. We do not . . . and we too often (*add specific prayers of confession*). In your mercy, forgive us. Let your light live in us that we may show forth your glory. We pray in Jesus' name. Amen."

Musical Notes: As the prayer concludes, band (or just piano) plays last line of refrain to cue congregation to begin singing stanza 3 and refrain.

RECONCILIATION

Liturgy Notes: Leader/liturgist says something like the following: "Jesus said: I am the light of the world, whoever follows me will not walk in darkness but will have the light of life (John 8:12). Friends, believe the good news: In Jesus Christ, we are forgiven!"

Musical Notes: A sustained keyboard can play gently in same key underneath the leader's words.

Silence is also fitting.

CELEBRATION

Musical Notes: "I Am the Light of the World" (GC 510). Key of E♭ (half step down from written music). Sing this Scripture song warmly and gently. Have soloists sing the refrain one time through before inviting the congregation to join in. Soloists may also sing all the stanzas, with the congregation joining only on the refrain.

Another great song to sing here is "The Lord Is My Saving Light," an upbeat gospel-style setting of Psalm 27. It's only available as a choir folio (GIA 3483). Key of E♭.

PREPARATION

Musical Notes: As the song concludes, have a solo instrument play the last phrase ("and a lamp unto my path") of the refrain of "Thy Word" (SNC 86) very freely and without accompaniment. Key of E♭. Then have the congregation join in singing this prayer for illumination. Sing twice through very slowly.

PROCLAMATION

Scripture: Philippians 2:12-18

Outline:

Introduction: story about trying to be "great"
1. Work out your own salvation.
    —it's hard work living a godly life
    —not works righteousness: work *out* salvation, not *for* salvation
    —it's God working in us
2. Work out . . . with fear and trembling.
    —not lest we lose it, but lest we dishonor it, not do it justice
    —we are to be witnesses, lights
3. Luminescence not our own.
    —illustration: kiddie stars on ceiling.
    —hold fast to the Word = dwelling in the light
    —our calling is to be like saints who glow with glory of God (Eastern Orthodox tradition)

Allow the sermon to conclude with a moment or two of silence, announced by the preacher.

Musical Notes: When the silence concludes (a minute or so), have a solo instrument play "This Little Light of Mine" (GC 513) very slowly, without other accompaniment, one time through in the key of C. This is a time for meditation and prayer. The congregation won't sing the song—not yet anyway.

DEDICATION

Musical Notes: "I Want to Walk as a Child of the Light" (SNC 77). Key of C. Keyboard and singers should lead on this childlike song of dedication. Let the adoration of the first three lines of the refrain soar before taking a small breath and praying the last line earnestly: "Shine in my heart, Lord Jesus."

INTERCESSION

Liturgical Notes: Leader offers prayers of intercession for the church and the world. Use light imagery as much as possible without being cloying. You may wish to use or adapt the prayer and sung refrain from *Sing! A New Creation* 206.

Musical Notes: "The Lord Is My Light" (SNC 206). Key of F. Sing with assurance. If you continue music underneath the spoken prayer, repeat the following progression: Dm, Dm7/C, B♭M7, Csus4, C. Go to C7 to cue the congregation to sing the refrain again.

DEDICATION

Liturgical Notes: Leader says something like the following: "God calls us to live in the light—and more than that, to *be* light to the world. 'Let your light shine before others,' Jesus says, 'so that others may see and give glory to God.' Let's commit ourselves now to live lives that glow with God's love: lives of justice, of tender love, of service to one another, of walking humbly with God. Let's offer our gifts to God."

Musical Notes: If the band plays anything under the spoken words above, it should be an unobtrusive transition into the key of G: F, walk the bass down to D (through E♭), Dsus, D7, then G. Then, while the leader is speaking, the band can play once through the refrain as an introduction to "We Are Called" (GC 718). Key of G (one step below printed music). This is an energetic song of dedication. Play in a moderate gospel groove, paying special attention to the triplets throughout. Snap the cutoffs, leaving the congregation, bass, and percussion alone to punch each "we are" of the refrain.

Then satisfy the desire to sing the most obvious of light-themed songs: "This Little Light of Mine." Key of G. Sing this spiritual as playfully and jubilantly as possible.

BENEDICTION

Liturgical Notes: Leader offers a benediction: "Congregational constellation, hear now the blessing of God: The Lord bless you and keep you; the Lord make his face to shine upon you and be gracious to you; the Lord lift up the light of his countenance upon you and give you peace. Amen."

Musical Notes: As the leader concludes, the band reprises "This Little Light."

Lent: Forgiveness

Matthew 18:21-35

Probably one of the most difficult parts of living a Christian life is rightly understanding and faithfully exercising the practice of forgiveness. It is at the heart of Christ's work. In his life, especially on the cross, Jesus absorbed evil without passing it on. We are called to follow him in this. To humbly ask for forgiveness, to graciously receive forgiveness, to gratefully grant forgiveness to others—these are lessons not mastered in a lifetime of discipleship.

So we return to the lessons regularly. The weeks during Lent—those forty days preceding Easter—are an excellent opportunity to explore the fundamentals of the Christian faith. One year at LOFT we used these weeks to do a sermon series on the Lord's Prayer. In this particular service, we explored Jesus' teaching that we ask God to "forgive our sins as we forgive those who sin against us." The service is structured to put into practice what we learn. Thus, the opening sequence of praise and adoration is abbreviated, and the sermon is immediately followed by the Lord's Prayer and then a confessional sequence with adequate time for silence and individual repentance.

CONGREGATION

Musical Notes: The service begins with a modern setting of parts of Psalm 84, "Better Is One Day" (MSP2 60). Key of E. The repetition in this song creates a rhythmic intensity expressing longing in the stanzas and finding fulfillment in the percussive refrain. The song can be meditative or celebrative—or in this case both. "My heart and flesh cry out" is urgent, pleading. "Better is one day" is exuberant. "I will draw near to you" becomes quieter, reverent, prayerful (see below). Let the guitars lead, using chords that let the high B and E strings ring. This gives the song a drone-like quality that can be enhanced using a sustained voice on a keyboard. If you use drums, ignore the snare and use the high-hat only to keep time. Make the most of your toms, playing strong sixteenth notes with appropriate accents throughout.

As the bridge concludes, the band goes to the coda, but the drums drop out, the singers don't sing, and everyone else is reverent while the leader/liturgist leads them in prayer.

Liturgical Notes: Leader, taking a cue from the lyric "we will draw near to you" begins prayer as the music continues underneath. "Lord Almighty, it is good to be here today in your house with your people. We love you, and we love to worship you. As we draw near to you, we pray that you will show us your beauty, that you will reveal to us your love. We ask that you will teach us how to live and how to pray. Make our hearts your home, your dwelling place, now and forever. Amen."

ADORATION

Musical Notes: When the prayer is done, the singers return to the start of the coda and lead the congregation softly singing again "Better Is One Day" Sing through the refrain another time or two. End, diminishing in volume and tempo.

Liturgical Notes: Leader says something like the following: "Listen to these words from God Almighty" and then reads from Isaiah 57:15. The first section should be read majestically.

Thus says the high and lofty one who inhabits eternity; whose name is Holy: I dwell in the high and holy place . . .

The next section should be read tenderly.

. . . and also with those who are contrite and humble in spirit, to revive the spirit of the humble, and to revive the heart of the contrite.

Musical Notes: As the liturgist reaches the word "humble," the band may begin softly to play an introduction to "Humble Thyself" (SPW 223). Key of Em. Sing antiphonally, men and women or congregational halves. Let the text guide your accompaniment/interpretation: humbly at first, then gradually more magnificent in tone. Sing the last time through humbly again, a cappella.

INTERCESSION

Liturgical Notes: Leader/liturgist says something like: "Let's turn humbly to God in prayer, lifting our souls, that God may lift us up."

A responsive reading of Psalm 25 follows. Keep explanation to a minimum: the leader can communicate all that is necessary with closed-eyed attention to the text while speaking and raised-brow attention to the congregation when they are to sing the refrain (see musical notes below).

Musical Notes: "To You, O Lord" (SNC 199). Key of D (half step down from written music). In this responsive setting of Psalm 25, the leader reads a few verses of the psalm (slowly and expressively), then the congregation sings the simple two-line refrain. Then a few more verses, the refrain again, and so on. Underneath the speaking, the accompaniment continues softly and smoothly, reflecting the character of the text being spoken or sung. For instance, "do not remember the sins of my youth" should have a confessional character while "All the paths of the Lord are steadfast love" should be more confident in tone. Always provide more congregational support on the refrain and make sure the band does not overpower the speaker on the verses.

Conclude by singing through the refrain at least two times.

Liturgical Notes: After the responsive reading, the leader may wish to offer a congregational prayer, using brief sentences of thanksgiving or petition like as follows: "God, we lift up in prayer El Salvador, the Middle East, and everywhere in the world where violence is the norm and your peace is desperately needed." Follow each petition with a sung refrain.

PREPARATION

Liturgical Notes: Leader concludes the time of prayer saying, "Lord, we lift our souls now to receive your Word. By the power of the Holy Spirit, give us eager ears, attentive minds, welcoming hearts, and supple wills. We pray in Christ's name. Amen."

PROCLAMATION

Scripture: Matthew 18:21-35

Outline:

The parable of the unforgiving servant.

Sermon could take either of two approaches:

- Straightforward doctrinal approach. Could use a classic statement of faith such as Heidelberg Catechism's Lord's Day 51. There are all sorts of wonderful books that plumb the depths of what it means to forgive and be forgiven: Lewis Smedes, *The Art of Forgiving*; L. Gregory Jones, *Embodying Forgiveness*.

- Narrative approach. Could follow the contours of the text. The jail images return again in the concluding hymn of this service ("And Can It Be").

Either way, the sermon should help the congregation understand *why* forgiveness is so central to the Christian life, *what* it means for him or her to be forgiven, and *how* to do it more intentionally, more graciously, more consistently. It should then conclude with the preacher leading the congregation in prayer.

INTERCESSION

Liturgical Notes: The Lord's Prayer

[If your congregation does not know the prayer by heart, print or project it for them. This also avoids awkward confusion over "trespasses" or "sins" and other small variations in how folks have learned it.]

Musical Notes: "Forgive Our Sins as We Forgive" (PsH 266). This contemporary hymn text is the perfect conclusion to a sermon on forgiveness. But the tune to which it's married here—from the Scottish Psalter of 1615—may not work for many congregations. I recommend using instead the familiar American folk tune LAND OF REST (SNC 249). Key of F. Play without a lilt, deliberately. Consider making use of an alternative harmonization, especially on the darker stanzas 2 and 3. One possibility would be to hold an F in the bass throughout and have a mid-range instrument repeatedly play down from D (D, C, B♭, A), one note per dotted quarter. Even darker is to walk down from C to A by half steps.

CONFESSION

Musical Notes: No musical transition is necessary to move directly into the explicitly confessional "Perdón, Señor" (SNC 59). Key of Dm. Acclimate the congregation to the gentle call and response by having a solo instrument play the melody of the "solo" part and the choir or lead singers sing the congregational response "forgive us, Lord." Since this pattern was introduced earlier in the service ("To You, O Lord"), they should have no trouble catching on after one pass through the song. A vocalist (or perhaps two contrasting voices, one male, one female) may sing the stanzas offered here (in English) interspersed with the congregation's penitent "perdón" (in English or Spanish). Note how the ending refrain circles right back without a break into the beginning refrain.

To extend and deepen the prayer, consider asking a spiritually sensitive wordsmith in your congregation to write a few additional stanzas before Sunday, the more specific and plain-spoken the better: "For yelling at our children, forgive us, Lord." "For selfish thoughts and actions, forgive us, Lord." Writing such stanzas would also make a great devotional exercise for the members of the band in the week before the service.

Liturgical Notes: As the song concludes, leader prays, "Merciful God, we come today asking your forgiveness. But we know we can't expect it unless we're willing to forgive others, to let go of the resentment we have for those who've hurt us. We pray for forgiveness, Lord. Hear our prayers, both the ones we know enough to say, and the ones we don't."

[Observe a time of silence—at least two minutes.]

Musical Notes: After a few minutes of silent prayer, the band may begin playing "Perdón" again. Repeat a few times with only the congregational response this time—no call or stanza. This gives members of the congregation a chance to think and quietly pray their own confessions. Conclude with a ritard and resolve not in Dm but D major (a picardy third). Go immediately into the next song.

RECONCILIATION

Musical Notes: "At the Cross" (SV4 10). Key of D (one step down from written music). Still confessional in tone, this song turns the gospel corner as it speaks of the cross as the place where "accused and condemned find mercy and grace." The movement in and out of key in the chorus signals the mixed emotions at being forgiven and recognizing its cost. Play with minimal accompaniment, intimately and prayerfully. A D7 chord at the conclusion will lead right into an introduction to the next song.

Liturgical Notes: As the introduction to the song begins, leader says, "Friends, Scripture tells us that Jesus bore our sins in his body on the cross so that we might be dead to sin and alive to all that is good. It tells us that Christ died for us while we were yet sinners, and that this is proof of God's amazing love—a love that declares this great good news: In Jesus Christ, you are forgiven. Let's thank God for that amazing, incomprehensible love!"

Musical Notes: "And Can It Be" (PsH 267). Key of G. Have the same minimal accompaniment (piano only?) play the refrain while the leader proclaims God's forgiveness. Add the rest of the band to cue the congregation to sing. Take a slower pace than usual—savor the rich text of this great hymn. Let your accompaniment aim at the wonder of the question "Can it be?"

You may wish choose a more contemporary musical setting for this text. Rev. Kevin Twit and the folks at the college ministry of Christ Community Church in Franklin, Tennessee, have put together two albums of classic hymns set to brand new singable tunes. The music—chords, lyrics, melody lines, recordings—is available at www.igracemusic.com. The guitar-driven version of "And Can It Be" on the album *Indelible Grace* is quite good. It's faster than you'd want at this point in the service, but slowed down a touch it would do well as an accompaniment to celebrate the implied response of God's "amazing love."

ADORATION/DEDICATION

Liturgical Notes: Leader says, "In return for all God has done for us, for all God has given and forgiven, let's sing praise and dedicate our lives to glorify and honor God."

Musical Notes: As the offering is received, the congregation sings "Amazing Love/You Are My King" (MSPW2 82). Key of D. Sing this prayer of dedication with joy and energy, somewhere around 70 bpm. Let the keyboards lead the congregation on the stanzas but then swell into the refrain and thicken the accompaniment with additional instruments and rhythmic subdivisions.

Liturgical Notes: Minister charges the congregation as follows: "As we leave, listen to these words from Scripture that help us to know how to live: Go out into the world in peace; have courage; hold on to what is good, return no one evil for evil; strengthen the fainthearted, support the weak, help the suffering, honor everyone; forgive others as you have been forgiven; love and serve the Lord, rejoicing in the power of the Holy Spirit."

BENEDICTION

Musical Notes: "My Friends, May You Grow in Grace" (SNC 288). Though I've suggested a number of other benediction songs in this collection of service plans, we almost always do this song at the conclusion of our services at LOFT. In fact, the first—and only—week we tried to conclude with another benediction, the congregation wouldn't leave. They stood, waiting expectantly for the opportunity to be blessed, to bless each other and glorify God with the same song they'd sung every other week. Even after the leader said "go in peace," they didn't go. Finally, above the discontented murmuring, someone in the back loudly demanded, "Play the song!" The band obliged, and we all learned a lesson about the need for ritual and predictability in worship, despite the contemporary craving for novelty. If not this song, find another way to do something exactly the same every week, to remind us of God's character of love, justice, and mercy—the same yesterday, today, and forever.

Easter

One of the gospel resurrection texts or 1 Corinthians 15

This energetic Easter service presumes two things. First, it presumes that the term "Alleluia" (literally, "God be praised!") has grown idle from congregational disuse during the season of Lent, as has been customary throughout much of the church's history. Second, it presumes that your congregation knows by heart the traditional liturgical responses of the Easter season: Alleluia! Christ is risen! **(Christ is risen indeed! Alleluia!)** If they don't, teach them winsomely, either with a bulletin announcement, with words projected overhead at the appropriate time, or with opening comments like the ones provided here.

CONGREGATION

Musical Notes: The service begins with "Celtic Alleluia" (SNC 148). Key of A. To start, set a brisk tempo, and have a minimal group (tom-tom drum and guitar or piano) softly repeat this two-bar chord pattern while the leader is speaking:
6/8 A - - A - - | A - - E - -.

Liturgical Notes:
[These opening comments are necessary only if your congregation is unfamiliar with the traditional Easter liturgical responses.]

While music plays underneath, leader says, "Christ is risen! Alleluia! We are an Easter people, amen? **(Amen)**. Today we celebrate Christ's resurrection. It is the linchpin of our lives. The center of everything. Our hope, our comfort, our joy—they're all compressed in a single sentence: Jesus is risen! Alleluia? **(Alleluia!)** Alleluia, he is risen indeed! For centuries, Christians have gathered on Easter and said these words to each other, to share the good news with each other and to give praise to God with our Alleluias. Today, throughout the world, millions of Christians are gathering. Wherever they meet, one will say to another, 'Alleluia! Christ is risen!' and the other will respond, 'Christ is risen indeed! Alleluia!' Let's try that together . . . *(responses)*. Great! Now, every time someone today says to you 'Christ is risen! Alleluia!' you're going to respond 'Christ is risen indeed! Alleluia!' Amen! Alleluia! Let's praise God together."

CELEBRATION

Musical Notes: When the speaker finishes opening comments (if they are used), bring in the rest of the band to play once through the refrain as an introduction to this rousing song of celebration. (See p. 35 for a description of an especially Celtic accompaniment for this song.) Otherwise, play the harmony as written and sing the Easter stanzas brightly and with unbounded joy. Percussive energy (from drums and/or guitar) and the descant played by a tin whistle or recorder really help the song soar. To end the song with a bang, don't slow down. Hold the last syllable while continuing the rhythmic accompaniment, and crescendo into an almost noisy shout of victory.

Note: Some congregations will not feel they have celebrated Easter without singing "Christ the Lord Is Risen Today" (PsH 388). Key of C. This classic hymn can be easily updated by having the guitars accompany using a syncopated rhythm: ♩ ♩ ♩

Other congregations will prefer the very new, very high-energy "My Redeemer Lives" (MSP2 73). Key of E♭.

Either of these may be sung at this point in the service instead of (or in addition to) "Celtic Alleluia." If you choose not to use "Celtic Alleluia" here, omit singing it below as well.

ADORATION

Liturgical Notes: Leader begins by leading the congregation in the traditional Easter responses, spoken with conviction and excitement: "Alleluia! Christ is risen!" (**"Christ is risen indeed. Alleluia!"**)

Leader then says something like the following: "Christ is the Son of God! Amen? He died and rose again! And he's here now with power to heal and grace to forgive. Do you believe it?"

Silence underneath these responses is best, but for a seamless transition from "Celtic Alleluia" to the next song, see musical note below.

PROFESSION

Musical Notes: If you wish to provide a seamless transition from "Celtic Alleluia" to the next song, ritard slightly and slowly play the following: A, A/G♯, F♯m7, Bsus, B7 underneath the spoken Easter responses above.

"I Believe in Jesus" (MSPW 7). Key of E, then F. This song is partly a declaration of belief and partly a prayer; partly a jubilant assertion of Christ's power and status and partly a recognition of his nearness in worship. Try to get at all these components. Dramatic accents on beats 1 and 2 in the first section give it a declarative force. Sustained chords, flowing lines and even tones in the second section ("I believe that he's here now") convey the mystery of his surrounding presence. After singing the song through, you may wish to skip the tag ending and transition up a notch into the key of F for a reprise of stanza 1. Simply play a C7 chord for the half measure before the congregation sings again.

ADORATION

Liturgical Notes: As the song concludes, leader says, "Lord, we believe in you, in your power, in your grace, in all you've done for us. We believe that you'll come again someday in glory. And we believe that you're here now. Help us to look for you. Help us to see you. Amen."

Musical Notes: If you want music to flow seamlessly throughout the service, have the pianist find a tempo while softly playing this transition: F, F/E, Dm7, Gsus, G7. That will bring you into the key of C for "Alleluia, He Is Coming" (SV4 10). The vocal range is odd on this song; some congregations sing with an octave leap going into the refrain, others stay on the same note. If the latter is the case with your congregation, you may prefer to leave the song in the key of G.

Sing slowly (♩ = 80), with wonder at Jesus' sacrifice and the mystery of God's presence among us. Support this pace with plenty of rhythmic texture on stanza 1 ("saw my Lord a-coming down the road").

CONFESSION

Musical Notes: Use less texture on the next two confessional stanzas. The refrains too should be subdued. After stanza 2 ("saw my Lord a-weeping for my sins"), continue playing very, very softly underneath a spoken prayer. One instrument (piano or guitar) would be plenty. Play no melody at all.

Liturgical Notes: After the refrain of stanza 2, before the last strains of "he is here" have died away, leader begins congregational prayer of confession as follows: "God of life, you sent your Son Jesus to us, but we confess that we don't often see him, and we certainly don't live as if we believe he is here. We . . . *(add prayers of confession, both personal and corporate, the more specific the better)*. We're often so filled with ourselves that there's no room for you. Forgive us, merciful God. Forgive the sin that sent Jesus to the cross."

Musical Notes: After the spoken prayer, sing stanza 3 sorrowfully ("saw my Lord a-dying on the cross"). Begin to see the hope of the resurrection in the two measures before stanza 4 ("saw my Lord a-rising from the grave"). Sing now with the splendor of new life. Bring back the texture and pick the tempo up just a tick. Repeat the refrain a second time, a cappella, if you wish.

REDEMPTION

Liturgical Notes: Leader says something like the following: "Scripture tells us this great good news: we have died with Christ, and we shall also live with him. We are now dead to sin—forgiven and freed—we are alive to God in Jesus Christ" (Rom. 6:8, 11, paraphrased). "His anger lasts only a moment, but his favor lasts a lifetime. Weeping may linger for the night, but joy comes with the morning. I can't be silent, I must sing for his joy has come!" (Ps. 30:5, 12, paraphrased).

Musical Notes: As the liturgist begins the passage from Psalm 30, the band introduces "Mourning into Dancing" (MMP3 298). Key of G. Have guitars go back and forth between G and C every two beats. The congregation begins singing not the refrain but the stanza. Sing with Easter euphoria. Give one full beat rest to let them know when to start. The song should dance with delight— encourage hand clapping, shoulder shaking, foot moving. Let the energy slow just a bit at "sweetness" and "morning sun." Then return to rollicking glee at "joyful gladness."

Without a break, begin the jubilant song "O Qué Bueno" (PsH 401). Key of D. Use an ensemble that resembles a mariachi band: strumming guitars, castanets, and a violin and trumpet playing in thirds. Sing in both English and Spanish.

PREPARATION

Liturgical Notes: Leader says, "We give you glory, Lord God, for salvation given to us in Jesus. We pray that the same power that raised him from the dead may break the grip of death in our lives and free our minds and hearts and wills to hear what you would say to us today. We pray in the name of Jesus Christ. Amen."

PROCLAMATION

Liturgical Notes: The service invites a fairly wide range of sermon directions, perhaps one of the classic resurrection texts from the gospels or 1 Corinthians 15, and would probably conclude with a note of celebration.

Musical Notes: After a brief introduction, sing—with the same brightness as before—the refrain of "Celtic Alleluia" twice through. For ease of transition, play in the key of F (two steps down from written music). At the concluding ritard, begin to feel it not in two, but in three. Hold the last chord for five beats (2 measures) and let the sixth serve as the pickup to "Alleluia, Alleluia! Give Thanks" (PsH 402). Key of F. Play this song not lightly as a simple children's song, but broadly, as an entry into deep thanksgiving and prayer.

INTERCESSION

Liturgical Notes: As the song concludes, leader offers prayers of thanksgiving and intercession on behalf of the congregation. Prayers of thanksgiving should come first. They should mention both universal and particular occasions for gratitude (both the glimpse of eternal life we see in Jesus and the gift of new life we see, for example, in the birth of a baby to a member of the congregation). Prayers of intercession also should also be both general and specific ("May we live each day in the light of your resurrection" as well as "We pray especially for _____, who now awaits her translation into glory. May she see with special clarity the hope of resurrection in you").

DEDICATION

Liturgical Notes: Leader invites the congregation to present their offerings to God as follows: "Now as we sing this simple 'Alleluia,' let's give to God out of gratitude for all he's given us."

Musical Notes: Sing a simple "Alleluia" here—something easy to learn that requires little mental or musical effort but invites one into meditative prayer and action. Perhaps the Taizé chant "Surrexit Christus" (GC 436). Key of D. Another good choice is the repetitive "Alleluia" (PsH 640), key of G. Or write your own. Pick a key signature, a time signature, a relaxed tempo, and use just a few chords.

CELEBRATION

Musical Notes: Conclude the service with thick, rich, uplifting praise. A wonderful hymn text set to an equally wonderful and familiar (yet underused) tune is "Alleluia, Jesus Is Risen" (SNC 150). Key of G (half step down from written music). Though guitars can add to the sound, a trumpet-enhanced accompaniment led by a keyboard is best. Then the congregation can sing with full-throated abandon. Stretch the last exultant Alleluia, and take a small breath between "lu" and "ia." As you attack the last chord, let the same ensemble that began the service (tom-tom drum, guitar), now with a melody instrument (penny whistle or violin) play once through the refrain of "Celtic Alleluia." Sing the three alternative "sending forth" stanzas, which are trinitarian in structure.

BENEDICTION

Liturgical Notes: Leader offers a benediction like the following: "The tomb is empty! Our lives are full." Christ is risen! Alleuia!" **(He is risen indeed! Alleluia!)**

"Now may the God of peace, who brought back from the dead our Lord Jesus, make you complete in everything good so that you may do God's will, working among us that which is pleasing in God's sight, through Jesus Christ, to whom be the glory forever and ever!" (Heb. 13:20, 21). **(Amen!)**

Musical Notes: You needn't use anything, but if you're looking for something to be sung as people leave, consider the light and infectious "Morning Sun" (TH 287). Key of A. Enjoy the toe-tapping strength of its "one-two" rhythm, but be careful that your drummer and bassist don't transform this song into a frivolous country-and-western sounding "boom-chick." Blues licks on the piano or guitars between sung phrases will help to steer you clear of danger.

Unless You Become Like Little Children

Matthew 18:1-4; 1 Corinthians 13:11; various Scripture stories

Although Superbowl Sunday is not a church holiday (literally, "holy day"), it is a cultural phenomenon whose influence North American churches have to deal with. Some churches lure sports lovers with free munchies and pre-game prayer, followed by projection of the big game on a big screen. My first year at Calvin, the students decided to go a different route. They wanted to offer a special service on Superbowl Sunday for people who weren't excited about men playing games on TV, but who *were* interested in being playful in other ways. Playfulness, they observed, is a characteristic of good worship that is best modeled by children. From that jumping-off point, we constructed a worship service based on the admonition to be "childlike, not childish." The key texts were Matthew 18:1-4 and 1 Corinthians 13:11.

This service is structured around a handful of childlike virtues (playful praise, expectancy, wonder, humility, openness, teachableness, honesty, intimacy, gratitude, trust). These building blocks were ordered to shape our time together, and mortared with Scripture lessons, children's songs, and slides based on the poignant and funny prayers found in the wonderful book *Children's Letters to God* (Workman Publishing Company, 1991).

Three additional notes:

- The service has a specific section for proclamation—a time of extended Bible-story telling—but preaching happens throughout as the worship leader guides the congregation through the liturgy, commenting on the songs, Scripture, and slides and connecting them to our lives. Follow this example or replace the more expository sections with testimony about God-given and childlike virtue wherever it's found.
- Involve children leading the service in as many ways as possible: playing musical instruments, singing, signing, teaching songs, offering prayers, reading Scripture or the letters to God.
- Almost all the songs used in this service are children's songs—well-known and well-loved (well, most of them). You won't find lots of innovative suggestions in this service plan for supporting the singing of songs like "Jesus Loves Me." It is enough to accompany the congregation in a childlike fashion: simply and honestly.

CONGREGATION

Musical Notes: The service begins with two responsorial songs. First, a sung call to worship from the psalms: "I Will Call upon the Lord" (SPW 224). Key of D.

Then "Hallelu, Hallelu, Hallelu, Hallelujah . . . Praise Ye the Lord" (SYL 88). Key of D. More popularly known as "the stand-up/sit-down song," these simple choruses of praise encourage the congregation—through the use of their bodies—to begin being playful in their worship.

Liturgical Notes: Leader says, "Praise ye the Lord!" **(Hallelujah!)**

"The Lord be with you." **(And also with you.)**

"It is good to be here giving praise to God. Today's service is going to be an experiment in childlikeness. In the gospel of Matthew, Jesus tells his disciples, who are wondering who's number one, that if they are to enter the kingdom of heaven they must become like children. (Matt. 18:3). But Scripture also says that we must 'put away childish things' (1 Cor. 13: 11). Today we'll be thinking about ways in which we can regain and retain the childlike features that prepare us to enter the kingdom of heaven, but also to put away childish things, both in worship and in our everyday lives.

"Frederick Buechner says, 'The people who get into heaven are people who, like children, don't worry about it too much. They are people who, like children, live with their hands open more than with their fists clenched. They are so unburdened by preconceptions that if somebody says there's a pot of gold at the end of the rainbow, they're perfectly willing to go take a look themselves' *(Wishful Thinking,* Harper San Francisco, 1993, p. 15).

"God has some surprises for us today. Let's worship with open hands."

Musical Notes: Sing "Father, I Adore You" (SFL 28). Key of F.

Liturgical Notes: Another leader/liturgist (perhaps a child) then leads in an opening prayer of adoration as follows: "Father, we adore you. We love you so much. You made the world and everything in it. You gave us Jesus to save us. You sent your Spirit to comfort us. We bless and praise you today. Help us to worship like little children, and to enter humbly into your kingdom. In Jesus' name. Amen."

Leader then says, "Children know that when we gather to worship, God is present among us. 'Where two or three are gathered in my name, I am there' says Jesus (Matt. 18:20). They expect God to be there. They expect to show God their new shoes."

Dear God, If you watch in church on Sunday I will show you my new shoes.

—Mickey

CELEBRATION

Liturgical Notes: Leader says, "Children know how to praise. They know it instinctively. They have an incredibly low "joy threshold." Without inhibition they play and pray and praise at the smallest thing. The first snowfall of the season will send a two-year-old into fits of delight: O snow! You make me so happy, snow! Thank you, God! They praise for no other reason than because God deserves it."

Dear God, I do not think anybody could be a better God. Well, I just want you to know but I am not just saying that because you are God.

—Charles

Musical Notes: Sing at least two songs of exuberant praise. If possible, connect with Scripture. For example, sing "Ain't No Rock" (SLK2) and connect with Luke 19:40. Other possibilities include the following: "I've Got the Joy, Joy, Joy, Joy, Down in my Heart," "Praise to the Lord, the Almighty" (SFL 27), "Shout to the Lord" (SNC 223).

ADORATION

Liturgical Notes: Leader says, "Children look at creation and know that it speaks of a good and loving God. The whole world, as Alexander Schmemann says, is transparent to the Divine. Children see, and know, and praise God for creation."

Dear God, it is great the way you always get the stars in the right places.

—Jeff

Dear God, I didn't think orange went with purple until I saw the sunset you made on Tue. That was cool.

—Eugene

Musical Notes: Sing a song of praise for creation: "All Things Bright and Beautiful" (SFL 90). Key of G. Go seamlessly into "Jesus Loves the Little Children." Key of G.

CONFESSION

Liturgical Notes: Leader says, "God made a beautiful creation and placed the people God loved so much in it. God told us to love each other as he loves us. But it's hard for us. We're so wrapped up in ourselves. We're selfish and full of pride. Our hearts are small—we don't even know how small, especially compared to God. Sometimes children can see more clearly than we can."

Dear God, I bet it is very hard for you to love all of everybody in the whole world. There are only four people in our family and I can never do it.

—Nan

63

Leader says, "Our love is often thin and shallow. And we don't like to admit responsibility for our sin. Adam blames Eve, Eve blames the snake, and we blame whoever or whatever is close at hand. Like children, we try to get out of the consequences of our actions. But we ought to know better."

Dear God, How do you know when you are old enough to know better?

—Marcie

Leader says, "What we need is a child's genuine humility—the humility to pray, to ask for forgiveness, to come to God with open hearts and hands. Let's pray together, singing these words from Psalm 51."

Musical Notes: While the leader speaks, the band begins playing an introduction to "Create in Me a Clean Heart" (SNC 49). Key of G. Sing twice through quietly, penitentially.

RECONCILIATION

Liturgical Notes: Leader says, "Even when a parent disciplines a child who has done wrong, the child doesn't doubt the parent's love. And children learn—sometimes quickly, sometimes not—that when they are contrite, a parent longs to forgive. So it is with God."

Leader reads Psalm 103:8-13:

8 The LORD is merciful and gracious, slow to anger and abounding in steadfast love. *9* He will not always accuse, nor will he keep his anger forever. *10* He does not deal with us according to our sins, nor repay us according to our iniquities. *11* For as the heavens are high above the earth, so great is his steadfast love toward those who fear him; *12* as far as the east is from the west, so far he removes our transgressions from us. *13* As a father has compassion for his children, so the LORD has compassion for those who fear him.

Musical Notes: "Jesus Loves Me" (SFL 61). Key of C. Sing all three stanzas, at least one a cappella.

Then transition (through C7) into the key of F in preparation for the next song, "Day by Day" (SFL 221). Key of F. (Or sing the same text to the tune made popular in the musical *Godspell*. Sing twice through.

Liturgical Notes: Leader says something like the following: "All God asks, in granting us forgiveness, is to say yes and then . . ."

Dear God, I am doing the best I can.

—Frank

". . . to do the best we can."

PREPARATION

Liturgical Notes: Leader says, "And we try to the best we can in our living and loving and learning. One of the things children do well is learning. Learning about life and about God. Childlike folk are eager to go to the Bible to learn the story of God's love and God's people. Children love to study the Bible, to ask questions . . ."

Dear God, I read the Bible. What does begat mean? Nobody will tell me.

Love, Alison

". . . to learn its stories and apply them to our lives . . ."

Dear God, Maybe Cain and Abel would not kill each other so much if they had their own rooms. It works with my brother.

—Larry

God: the bad people laghed at noah—you make an ark on dry land you fool. But he was smart he stuck with you. That's what I would do.

—Eddie

Leader (or child) prays as follows: "God, we thank you for the Bible. Help us to listen and really hear what you say to us in it. In Jesus' name. Amen."

PROCLAMATION

Liturgical Notes: Here simple Scripture stories may be read—ones that need little explanation. Tell favorites from the Old and New Testaments.

Musical Notes: If you wish, you may also wish to sing some of the following Bible story songs: "Arky/Rise and Shine," "Who Built the Ark?" (SFL 99), "Dare to Be a Daniel" (SFL 104), "Joshua Fought the Battle of Jericho" (SFL 106), "Only a Boy Named David" (SFL 109), "Zacchaeus Was a Wee Little Man" (SFL 115)," I Cannot Come" (*Joy Is Like the Rain,* Medical Mission Sisters).

LAMENTATION

Liturgical Notes: Leader says, "When we are childlike we can be honest. Because we know the story of God and God's people—because we know God intimately, like Moses and David and Peter—we can come to God in prayer with our truest selves. Our angry or puzzled or mournful selves."

Reader (a child)—reads Ps. 22:11: "Do not be far from me, for trouble is near and there is no one to help."

Dear God, Fourth grade is even harder than third grade. Does that keep going on?

—Denise

God, did you really mean do unto others as they do unto you, because if you did then I'm going to fix my brother.

—Darla

Dear God, Please send Dennis Clark to a different camp this year.

—Peter

Leader says, "Often our prayers are childish, not childlike. We are concerned with ourselves, and we ask God for stuff we want. Just stuff we want."

Dear God, Please send me a pony I never ask for anything before you can look it up.

—Bruce

I wrote you before, do you remember? Well, I did what I promised but you didn't send the pony yet.

—Louis

Leader says, "On the other hand, children often pray with great sensitivity about the world's hurts because they are so close to God's heart. They know what breaks it."

Dear God, I wish you would not make it so easy for people to come apart. I had 3 stitches and a shot.

—Janet

Dear God, Instead of letting people die and having to make new ones why don't you just keep the ones you got now?

—Jane

INTERCESSION

Liturgical Notes: Leader says, "With childlike honesty and sensitivity, let us pray together." Then leader or a child (or series of children) offers a prayer for the congregation and the world.

You may wish to divide the spoken prayer up into sections and sing a prayer response in between each section. Or conclude the entire prayer with one of the suggested sung prayer songs.

Musical Notes: "Lord, Listen to Your Children Praying" (SFL 54), "Kum Ba Yah" (SFL 53). Key of C.

DEDICATION

Liturgical Notes: Leader says, "Prayer comes easily to children. They don't fill their lives with so many things that there's no room for God. They have a natural gift for practicing the presence of God. . . .

Dear God, I think about you sometimes even when I'm not praying.

—*Elliott*

"They know God is always with them."

Dear God, I don't ever feel alone since I found out about you.
—*Nora*

Leader says, "To be childlike is to long to be close to God, and to be grateful, even when things don't quite go your way."

Dear God, Thank you for the baby brother. But what I prayed for was a puppy.
—*Joyce*

Dear God, What does it mean You are a Jealous God? I thought you had everything.
—*Jane*

Reader (a child) prays a prayer of thanksgiving and dedication as follows: "Dear God, thank you for everything you let us borrow. Help us to remember that everything really belongs to you and not us. In Jesus' name, amen."

Then leader says, "As we sing this prayer, let's present to God our gifts and offerings and commit ourselves to living for Jesus."

Musical Notes: Sing a song of dedication and/or thanksgiving such as the following: "In My Life, Lord" (SFL 71), "Thank You for Giving Me the Morning" (SYL 49), "Father, We Adore You" (SFL 77), "Give Thanks" (SNC 216).

You could also sing "Lord, I Want to Be a Christian" (SFL 40) and alter the lyrics to reflect the childlike virtues held up in this service: Lord, I want to be more playful, be more humble, be more trusting, be more honest, and so on.

CELEBRATION

Liturgical Notes: Leader says, "Finally, to be childlike is to trust that no matter what, God is in control. God watches and guards us so that not a hair can fall from our heads without God knowing about it. To be childlike is to play at life with abandon, for that is our destination when our world is finally brought to its full redemption.

Reader (a child) reads Zechariah 8:3-5:

3 Thus says the LORD: I will return to Zion, and will dwell in the midst of Jerusalem. . . . *4* Old men and old women shall again sit in the streets of Jerusalem. . . . *5* And the streets of the city shall be full of boys and girls playing in its streets.

God, you don't have to worry about me. I always look both ways.

—*Dean*

Musical Notes: Sing "He's Got the Whole World in His Hands" (SFL 198).

BENEDICTION

Liturgical Notes: Leader says, "To be childlike is to trust God's Word: that God will bring to completion the good work God began in us (Phil. 3), to bring us all—old folks and babies and everyone in between—to the full maturity of the knowledge of the love and grace of God (Eph. 4:13). Amen.

"Go now in peace to love and serve the Lord."

Musical Notes: Sing a closing song: "Amen, siakudi misa" (SNC 287), "Shalom" (SFL 84).

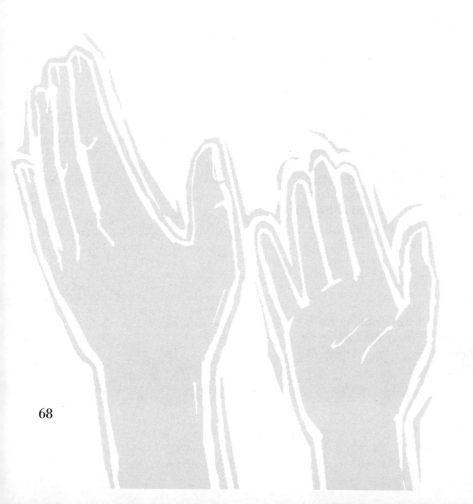

Lord's Supper: Abiding and Feasting on Love

John 15:1-17

The theme of love is full of richness, but it's tricky. It's easy for worship planners to just pick songs with the word "love" figuring prominently in the lyrics. Trouble is, that doesn't guarantee much liturgical balance. Depending on the fields from which you harvest songs for worship, you may end up with 90 percent upbeat tunes expressing our love for God, and nothing about God's love for others, or God's love for us, or what that love cost, or how it comes to us in Jesus. Nothing about how we abide in God's love and then bear fruit, that love flowing, by God's grace and the Spirit's power, through us to our neighbors.

No one can pack all that in to a handful of songs. Even toss in a substantial sermon on a rich passage (John 15:1-17), and we're still just nibbling around the edges. Fortunately, worship at its best is much more than spoken and sung words. We have other another means of grace, another way to encounter God—the sacraments, particularly the Lord's Supper.

This service, then, provides a liturgy for the celebration of communion. Note that the song choices clearly reflect that it is a *celebration,* not only a solemn commemoration. The language is updated and streamlined so that it doesn't feel too wordy for congregations impatient with traditional liturgical forms. It is simple enough that a pastor can (and perhaps should) memorize it.

Musically, this service plan offers greater choice than the others in this book. That's especially true for the section of the service where the congregation actually eats and drinks the bread and wine. Consequently, it's impossible to provide instructions for seamless transitions, which often depend upon key modulations and transpositions. You'll find that nearly every song has been left in the key in which it's written. Musical transitions between songs in different keys will need to be made quickly and confidently in order to sustain momentum. Don't be afraid of sonic white space in worship—intentional stillness is an underappreciated blessing. But do avoid the awkward and purposeless "what's happening now" sort of silence. Try to have a music page-turner at your keyboardist's side, and trade off introductions between the guitar and the piano.

CONGREGATION

Musical Notes: A lone guitar begins, quietly but insistently, an introduction to "Gather Us In" (SNC 8). Key of D. Strum sixteenth notes, but mute with the right hand all but beats 1 and 4. A low tom tom may gently join the call to worship. Go through the song one full time as the congregation attends to the leader.

Liturgical Notes: Over the introduction, the leader says, "God, speaking through the prophet Jeremiah, speaks to us today: 'I have loved you with an everlasting love; I have drawn you with loving-kindness. This is what the Lord says: I will bring them from the land of the north and gather them from the ends of the earth.' (Jer. 31:3, 7, 8).

"Let's pray together. . . ."

ADORATION

Musical Notes: Cue the congregation to sing by bringing in the rest of the band—piano, maybe a woodwind. Be careful not to play so fast that the words are lost in a melodic muddle. End the song with a slowing double tag (ritard as you repeat the last line twice). Then have the piano play a rhythmless transition into the key of F: D/C, B♭, B♭/A, Gm7, C7sus, C7. Hold that chord, anticipating even more praise.

Out of this expectant sound the guitar begins, in tempo, the repeated four-chord lick (F2, Gm7[4], Bb2, C7sus) that serves as an introduction to "I Could Sing of Your Love Forever" (MSPW2 63). Key of F. Let the guitars lead this song throughout. While its stanzas are a bit obscure, "I Could Sing" has an infectious chorus, powerful in its simplicity. After the bridge, pull out all the stops and sing with abandon, even of the "foolish" sort the lyric talks about. Then sing the chorus once more a cappella.

Enjoy a breath of stillness before the piano begins playing the introduction to "The Power of Your Love (MSPW 26). Key of G. Accompany with piano alone, pleading, on the stanzas. Then add the rest of the band, crescendoing into the soaring confidence of the refrain. Snap off at "you," slow down, and allow only the guitar to support the congregation as the song ends.

Another possibility at this point in the service would be to sing the very popular "Shout to the Lord" (SNC 223). Key of A.

CONFESSION

Musical Notes: Again, a solo piano provides the introduction to the next song, "My Jesus, I Love Thee" (PsH 557). Key of E♭. Sing and play the first stanza with contrition ("for thee all the follies of sin I resign"). The drums, if you have them, may drop out altogether, but if you can, add a solo instrument on melody. When the stanza is done, leader will begin to speak. Drop in volume while continuing to play through one stanza of the song. Avoid the melody while the "silent" prayer is offered.

Liturgical Notes: Jumping in before the fourth beat of the last measure (to keep the congregation from going on), leader offers a prayer of confession as follows: "Merciful God, you love us, we know. But we do not love you fully. You call, but we don't always listen. We walk away from those in need. We condone wickedness. We hold you at arm's length, despite the lengths you went to, to keep us close to you. Forgive us, Lord. We offer you our silent prayers of confession."

[Observe silence until the stanza concludes and the band modulates up to the next key.]

REDEMPTION

Musical Notes: At the end of the silent prayer, modulate up to the key of F. Hold the last note ("now") for two beats (not four), then C7 for two beats.

As the leader testifies to God's love and assures the congregation of forgiveness (below), play through the stanza once more, this time more brightly—and in a new key (add a guitar strumming a chord every half note). Still, avoid a melody.

Liturgical Notes: Leader (again, jumping in before the congregation expects to sing) pronounces God's forgiveness with words adapted from Ephesians 1: "Praise be to the God and Father of our Lord Jesus Christ, who chose us before the creation of the world to be holy and blameless in his sight. In love he predestined us to the praise of his glorious grace freely given us in the One he loves. Because of Jesus Christ we have redemption through his blood—the forgiveness of sins."

Musical Notes: Then sing stanzas 2 and 4 of the hymn, intensifying the triumphant character of the song to its conclusion in paradise ("in mansions of glory"). Sustain the last chord by playing a B♭/F, then go straight ahead to adore God with "I Love You, Lord" (SNC 16). Key of F. Sing through twice, accompanied the first time, a cappella the second. Enjoy the fetterless praise, but have your vocal leaders keep the tempo moving, lest it become too maudlin.

PREPARATION

Liturgical Notes: Leader prays as follows: "O Lord, we love you. We want our praise to be as sweet to you as your Word is to us. We need you. We don't live by bread alone. Your Word sustains us. Your love keeps us alive. Feed us now. We pray in Jesus' name, amen."

PROCLAMATION

Scripture: John 15:1-17

Outline: I am the vine.

Introduction: What is fruit like?

A. How can we be fruitful? "Abide in me"

    1. Like words we say to each other, let my words live in you—let Scripture sink in, find a heart-home.

2. Keep my command: Love one another as I have loved you.
   —Difficult to literally lay down life, but lots of little ways.
   —You are my friends—share what's most important.
   —Natural outcome of "abiding"—don't worry about it.
B. Why should we be fruitful?
   1. When we don't love, we wither.
   2. When we don't love, we become useless, thwarting God's will.
   3. When we love, we glorify God
   4. Self-interest: we get what we ask for (in Christ's name).
   5. Fullness of joy—paradox that painful path leads to life.

Sermon concludes with a prayer.

After the prayer, you may observe a moment of silence.

DEDICATION

Musical Notes: After the moment of silence, the band begins to play an introduction to the next song, "We Have Been Told" (SNC 136). Key of D. Use primarily piano, supplemented by a finger-picked guitar. You may wish to have this song sung by a soloist rather than by the congregation.

Liturgical Notes: During the introduction to the next song, leader says, "As we sing (or listen), you are invited to present your gifts to God."

While the congregation sings, the offering is either collected or brought forward by the individual congregants and placed in common baskets.

PRESENTATION

Liturgical Notes: If the offering wasn't brought forward by the congregants during the song, bring it forward to the table on the final stanza. Then have a family in the congregation come forward and place on the table the bread and wine to be used for the celebration of the Lord's Supper.

Musical Notes: Another possibility right after the sermon is to sing a different scriptural song that has to do with love. For example, a lovely setting of 1 Corinthians 13 is the contemporary hymn "Not for Tongues of Heaven's Angels" (SNC 275), key of A♭.

Other options include the simple and reflective "Oh, How He Loves You and Me" (SFL 163). Key of A. Or begin to focus on the Lord's Supper by singing a song of invitation as the elements are brought forward—the warm and welcoming "Table of Plenty" (SNC 247), key of D; or the Caribbean-flavored "The Feast Is Ready to Begin" (WPS 139), key of G.

INTERCESSION

Liturgical Notes: The communion service begins with a brief explanation of the sacrament, and then the "Great Prayer of Thanksgiving." The *Didache* (literally, "teaching"), the ancient church writing from which most communion liturgy is based, recommends that the leader extemporize a prayer before celebrating the Lord's Supper. But if the leader can't, it says, a reasonable option is to say words like the following:

"Dear friends of Jesus Christ, the holy Supper we are about to celebrate is a feast of remembrance, of communion, and of hope. We come in remembrance that Jesus took our sin upon himself and died the bitter and shameful death on the cross in order to save us from our sin. We come to have communion with this resurrected Christ—in the elements of bread and wine, and in our fellowship with all Christians who are members of the one Body. We come in hope, believing that this bread and cup are a promise and foretaste of the feast of love of which we shall all partake when his kingdom has fully come, when we shall see him, and each other, face to face.

"Come! Let us feast together!"

Leader then begins following prayer of Thanksgiving (congregation stands):

"The Lord be with you."
(And also with you.)
"Lift up your hearts."
(We lift them to the Lord.)

"It is right, our duty and our delight, that we should at all times and in all places give thanks to you, O holy Lord, Father almighty, eternal God.

"We praise you that you . . . *(pastor offers a prayer of thanks—a resumé of salvation—that ties directly into Scripture/theme of the week).*

"Therefore, with the whole company of saints in heaven and on earth, we worship and glorify you, and we sing with joy."

Musical Notes: The opening words of the sacrament may be spoken by the pastor as indicated above, or they may be sung. To do the latter, have the piano or guitar introduce "Lift Up Your Hearts unto the Lord" (PsH 309). Key of Dm (a step up from written music). Sing with energy.

Let the last chord (Dm) ring.

Then go right into the "Sanctus" a song that celebrates God's holiness. I suggest the Brazilian-influenced "You Are Holy" (SNC 20). Key of Dm. Feel this light samba in two. Sing through once, then divide the congregation in half and sing as a round. Use lots of percussion throughout.

Other options for the "Sanctus" include the intimate Argentinian "Santo" (SNC 19), key of C; the insistent "Lord of the Heavens" (HMC), key of Dm; the ethereal "We Fall Down" (MSPW2 66), key of E; the familiar "Holy Holy Holy Is the Lord of Hosts" (SPW 35), key of C; or stanza 1 of the classic hymn "Holy Holy Holy" (PsH 249), key of D.

INSTITUTION

Liturgical Notes: Pastor says, "We give thanks that the Lord Jesus, on the night of his arrest, took bread, and after giving thanks to God, he broke it, and said, 'This is my body, given for you. Do this in remembrance of me.' *(Breaks bread while speaking.)*

"In the same way, he took the cup after supper, saying, 'This cup is the new covenant sealed in my blood. Whenever you drink it, do it in remembrance of me.'" *(Pours cup.)*

INVOCATION/INTERCESSION

Liturgical Notes: Pastor leads congregation in prayer as follows: "Gracious God, pour out your Holy Spirit upon us that this bread and this cup may be for us the body and blood of our Lord, and that we, and all who share this feast, may be one with Christ and he with us. Fill us with eternal life, that with joy we may be his faithful people until we feast with him in glory. *(may include here petitions for the life of the congregation)* For it is in the name of Jesus Christ your servant that we pray *(may lead the congregation in the Lord's Prayer)*. Amen."

INVITATION

Liturgical Notes: Pastor continues as follows: "People of God, this table has been prepared for all who love and trust in God for their salvation. We come not because we ought, but because we may. Not because we are righteous, but because we are penitent. Not because we are strong, but because we are weak. Not because we are whole, but because we are broken. Come then, for all is ready *(holds up the bread and cup)*. The gifts of God for the people of God!"

COMMUNION

Musical Notes: Worship leaders should provide music during communion. Music helps bring the wandering spirit home and amplifies the sensitivity of the focused soul. Since there's no telling now long it will take all the members of the congregation to eat and drink, the well-prepared worship team has a series of songs ready to go—as many as are needed. While an incredibly astute worship leader can sense where the congregation is and where it needs to go next, and can choose songs to fit the circumstances, the rest of us need more modest goals: select and prepare a half dozen songs of varied types. Some of the music should be textually rich—a hymn or substantive folk song. Some should be simple and meditative. Some should be sung by the congregation, and some for it. Some should be faster, some slower; some newer, some older. Following is a sampling of some of the best stuff that's out there, listed under a variety of categories:

The "Latest Thing": Earnest and intimate

"Precious Jesus/I Remember You" (CH 33). Key of A. A textually rich and moving memorial of Christ's sacrifice. Use sustained chords played by keyboards or other instruments to create a sonic bath. Let the melody float in on the 6/8 waves.

"Holy and Anointed One" (MSPW 32). Key of G.

"Amazing Love/You Are My King" (MSPW2 82). Key of D.

Simple and meditative

Eat this Bread (SNC 254). Key of G. One of the most well-known of the songs from the Taizé community in France. Sing in an unhurried, comforting, reflective tone. Make extensive use of the descants, though the solo stanzas may be omitted.

"God Is Love" (SNC 137). Key of D.

"Father, I Adore You" (SFL 28). Key of F.

"Oh, How He Loves You and Me" (SFL 163). Key of A.

Classic hymns

"Oh, the Deep, Deep Love of Jesus" (MPCB4 229). Key of Em. It may jar some congregations, but the sense of the "rolling, mighty ocean" of God's love can be effectively embodied in the sonic texture of an electric guitar with the distortion turned way up. Walk the bass down from E to B on the measure before each stanza begins.

"Beautiful Savior" (PsH 461) Key of E♭.

"Love Divine" (PsH 568). Key of F.

Folk songs

"Soul, Adorn Yourself with Gladness/Vengo a ti, Jesús amado" (LLC 388) Key of Am. Let a soloist (and another voice for the alto part) sing this lovely prayer from South America. The passionate, almost romantic flavor of the tune exactly fits the ancient text and its use of the metaphor of Christ as our bridegroom. The song can also be found in Reformed Worship 66 (December 2002).

"We Have Been Told" (SNC 136). Key of D.

"Table of Plenty" (SNC 247). Key of D.

"Not for Tongues" (SNC 275). Key of A♭ (a possibility above too).

"Bless the Lord, O My Soul" (PsH 627). Key of E♭.

Upbeat songs

"Taste and See" (SNC 255). Key of F. A good-natured gospel setting of Psalm 34.

"The Feast Is Ready" (WPS 139). Key of G. (see also above).

"Let Us Talents" (SNC 258). Key of C. Another Caribbean influenced song.

Liturgical Notes: Congregants come forward to receive the bread and wine in one of two ways:

- They gather in a small circle around the table and serve each other. As the elements come around the circle, they break off a piece of bread and dip it into the cup, saying to each other, "This is Christ's body, given for you" or "Jesus loved you so much that he poured out his life for you in this cup."
- The congregation comes forward, single file, to where the minister and other church leaders are standing, holding bread and cup. Each member eats and drinks as the leader says appropriate words. They then return to their seats by another way.

All the while, other members of the congregation are singing.

CELEBRATION

Liturgical Notes: Leader says something like the following: "The Lord has fed us at the banquet table! Let us sing his praise!"

Musical Notes: The traditional conclusion to a Lord's Supper meal is a setting of Psalm 103. A few options are the gospel-influenced "Bless the Lord, O My Soul" (PsH 627), key of E♭ (mentioned above); two hymn settings: "Praise My Soul the King of Heaven" (PsH 475), key of D and "O Come, My Soul" (PsH 297), key of B♭; and the Taizé "Bless the Lord, My Soul" (SNC 256). For this service, try the jubilant "His Banner over Us" (SV3 62). Key of C. A simple and celebratory tune coupled with a text based on the Song of Solomon.

INSTRUCTION

Liturgical Notes: Leader says, "Go into the world in peace. Love the Lord your God with all your heart, with all your soul, and with all your mind. And this too: Love your neighbor as yourself. Everything hangs on these two commandments."

Musical Notes: As leader concludes the charge, an electric guitar begins a driving introduction to "They'll Know We Are Christians" (GC 735). Key of Em (half step down from written music). Usually a little too self-congratulatory for corporate worship, this song works here because of the doxological last stanza and because of the context of God's love, which enables and stimulates our love for God and for each other.

BENEDICTION

Liturgical Notes: Leader says, "The love of God, the grace of Jesus Christ, and the fellowship of the Holy Spirit be with us all. Amen."

RECESSIONAL

Musical Notes: "Now Go in Peace" (SNC 289). Key of G. This island-tinged song is especially fitting if the first song in the communion sequence was "The Feast Is Ready" and the last was "Let Us Talents and Tongues Employ." Once the congregation knows it, sing as a round as you recess with joy.

Ten Service Plans
for
Contemporary
Worship

Ron Rienstra models for Calvin's student worship leaders a ferocious commitment to think carefully *about* God—thus, sturdy theology—and at the same time a fresh eagerness to explore things new and old as raw material for the worship *of* God. Each week at Calvin's LOFT and Jazz Vespers I see a new generation learning to sing the Lord's song faithfully and well. And when I do, I am glad all over again.

Dale Cooper, Chaplain, Calvin College, Grand Rapids, Michigan

Ten Service Plans helps worship planners assemble the crucial pieces of historic God-encounter into seamless, culturally compelling designs. Like worship Legos with detailed assembly instructions. What a concept!

Sally Morgenthaler, Author, *Worship Evangelism,* Founder, Sacramentis.com

These straightforward service plans speak to the dearth of adequate instruction in and modeling of how to make transitions to and from the various parts of a worship service. Very helpful and much needed.

Scott Harrison Coil, Campus Ministries Worship Research Assistant,
Seattle Pacific University, Seattle, Washington

The fruit of Ron's commitment to frankness and genuine community, his tenacity in asking tough questions of every facet of worship, and his thoughtful synthesis of the best of a wide variety of Christian traditions are evident in these services. They combine a high degree of artistic style with an uncompromising measure of theological substance.

Gregg de Mey, Minister of Music,
Granite Springs Christian Reformed Church, Rocklin, California

Ron Rienstra is Associate for Student Worship at Calvin College, Grand Rapids, Michigan, and directs the LOFT, student-planned and -led worship at Calvin College. He writes two columns in the quarterly journal *Reformed Worship,* "What's on the Web" and "Notes from the LOFT"—these ten service plans are an expansion of his popular column on the LOFT. Rienstra is a graduate of Princeton Theological Seminary and is an ordained minister in the Reformed Church in America.

FAITH ALIVE® Christian Resources
www.FaithAliveResources.org
1-800 333-8300

www.calvin.edu/worship
1-616-957-6088

ISBN 1-56212-868-X

9 781562 128685